The Welfare Family and Mass Administrative Justice

Daniel J. Baum

Published in cooperation with
the Center for Administrative Justice
of the American Bar Association

The Praeger Special Studies program—
utilizing the most modern and efficient book
production techniques and a selective
worldwide distribution network—makes
available to the academic, government, and
business communities significant, timely
research in U.S. and international economic, social, and political development.

The Welfare Family and Mass Administrative Justice

PRAEGER SPECIAL STUDIES IN U.S. ECONOMIC, SOCIAL, AND POLITICAL ISSUES

Praeger Publishers   New York   Washington   London

Library of Congress Cataloging in Publication Data

Baum, Daniel Jay.
    The welfare family and mass administrative justice.

    (Praeger special studies in U.S. economic, social,
and political issues)
    1. Public welfare—United States—Law.   2. Children
—Law—United States.   3. Administrative procedure—
United States.   I. Title.
KF3720.5.B3   362.8'2'0973   74-11598
ISBN 0-275-09420-0

PRAEGER PUBLISHERS
111 Fourth Avenue, New York, N.Y. 10003, U.S.A.
5, Cromwell Place, London SW7 2JL, England

Published in the United States of America in 1974
by Praeger Publishers, Inc.

Printed in the United States of America

ACKNOWLEDGMENTS

An earlier draft of this book was prepared for a conference of highly selected persons sensitive to the problems of mass administrative justice and welfare hearings. Both in the earlier draft and from the conference there came critique of the work. Many of the nearly eighty persons who attended the conference provided material, insight, and analysis in correspondence, telephone conferences, and personal interviews. At the conference itself, a draft of this work was discussed by the plenary session. Accordingly, I thank all of the conference participants.

There were, however, certain individuals who gave added assistance. They include: R. K. Best, then Deputy Director, California Department of Social Welfare; Joel Cohen, Assistant General Counsel, Social Rehabilitation Service, Social Security Administration; Henry A. Freedman, Director, Center on Social Welfare Policy and Law; Mitchell I. Ginsberg, Dean, School of Social Work, Columbia University; Richard Greenberg, Center on Social Welfare Policy and Law; Felix Infausto, Deputy Commissioner, New York State Department of Social Services; Donna Kirchheimer, Human Resources Administration, New York City; Joel Robin, Assistant Attorney General, Maryland; Edward V. Sparer, Professor, School of Law, University of Pennsylvania; Ronald Zumbrunn, Special Counsel, Social and Rehabilitation Service, Department of Health, Education and Welfare.

In addition, I thank my research assistant, Judith Brav Sher, M.S.W. The Center for Administrative Justice, through its Executive Director, Milton Carrow, and its Board, read drafts and provided constructive critique for this book. To them I also extend my thanks, but as must be the situation, I assume full responsibility for the work itself.

CONTENTS

LIST OF TABLES

INTRODUCTION
by Milton M. Carrow

For its first major project, the Center for Administrative Justice embarked on an in-depth examination of the "fair hearing" process in the administration of the categorical welfare program of aid to dependent children. Recognized as a prime example of "cooperative federalism" by virtue of the interaction of federal and state agencies, it opened, for the Center, a Pandora's box of problems, revealing in microcosm practically all of the complexities of what is becoming known as "mass administrative justice."

The project, so far, has had three phases. The first was the commissioning of Professor Daniel J. Baum, the author of this volume, to prepare an analytic study of the subject and to assemble other pertinent materials. These were used as background materials for the second phase, a conference called by the Center in cooperation with the University of Virginia Law School, in June 1973 at Charlottesville, Virginia. In revised form, such background materials constitute the present book. The third step was the conduct of a pilot professional training seminar for welfare hearing officers.

The conference was attended by 60 participants—administrators, academics, and lawyers in the fields of welfare administration, administrative law, political science, and social work. To avoid exacerbation of the apparently polarized views between administrators on the one hand and recipient groups and their representatives on the other, a careful effort was made to have representation of the differing positions, leavened by the presence of the less embattled academics and generalists. Except for two minor eruptions during the two-day sessions, the workshops, panels, speeches, and so forth moved flowingly.

The pilot professional training seminar was conducted at the George Washington University in Washington, D.C., in January 1974, under the direction of Professor Robert E. Park. It was attended by 28 welfare hearing officers, both lawyers and nonlawyers, from 21 states. They were furnished with a 250-page manual and other materials prepared expressly for the seminar, and they spent four intensive days examining the problems of the fair hearing process, exchanging views and methodologies, studying training techniques, and participating in round-table discussions on how to improve the system and its personnel.

Milton M. Carrow is Director of the Center for Administrative Justice.

viii

From the foregoing there emerged an identification, if not more, of the kinds of problems that confront the welfare adjudicative processes. Since many of these problems also have implications for other areas of mass administrative justice, the present publication seems well warranted. Professor Baum's text deals with the subject in detail in light of statutes, cases, regulations, and practices. Here I will note some of the pertinent observations by the participants of the conference and the professional seminar.[1] But before indicating the problems discussed, a word about mass administrative justice.

MASS ADMINISTRATIVE JUSTICE

Like other important phenomena, mass administrative justice has had an unrecognized existence for some time, as, for example, in the adjudication of claims for social security benefits and veterans benefits. Its distinguishing characteristics are (1) the massive numbers of adjudicative proceedings to be dealt with, as its name implies, and (2) perhaps more important, the fact that in many of these matters the government is the dispenser and provider—rather than the regulator—of funds, services, or the distribution of goods.

As I have said elsewhere, ". . . the quantitative aspect is manifest from the growth, in recent years, of many new areas of administrative power, such as in the fields of health, welfare, public housing, education, environmental protection, parole and prisoner grievances, safety, land use, and most recently, energy control. The numbers of adjudicative determinations that have to be made in these areas are legion, and they affect the most vital aspects of an individual's day-to-day affairs."[2]

Also, ". . . since in the past the main concern of administrative law has been with the nature and process of government regulation of private activity, are the same principles to be applied where the government itself is the producer of funds, services and materials (welfare payments, food stamps, school lunches, farm subsidies, housing, schooling)?"[3]

TYPES OF PROBLEMS

The general subjects under which the different problems in the welfare administrative process focus are the hearing officer, the hearing system, and the checks on the officer and the system.

The Hearing Officer

The main questions regarding hearing officers have to do with qualifications and role. Should they be required to be lawyers, or can social workers and administrators perform the function as well or better? Are lawyers inclined to be formalistic and social workers compassionate? Is due process a special domain of lawyers?

To illustrate the unique nature of some of these problems, there was the story, presented to the seminar participants, of the elderly lady who was notified that her welfare payments were to be reduced on the ground that she had outside sources of income. She appeared at a hearing to challenge this charge and asserted that her payments should be continued because she had terminal cancer. Although this was not "relevant" and not a part of the record, most of the lawyer and nonlawyer participants thought this factor should be considered.

Related to such problems is the question of "sensitizing" the hearing officer to the full scope of his role. Often, it is said, he "wears three hats," for he is not only the adjudicator, but also, where the recipient does not have counsel, which is most of the time, he must function in such capacity, and where the agency has not brought counsel, he must fill that role too. The question then arises, by what means can it be established that a hearing officer has such judicious qualifications? And also, can training programs be offered which can develop the needed awareness and capacity?

The states of New York and California require their hearing officers to be lawyers. Other states do not. If nonlawyers are used, should they be required to be trained in the nature and elements of the hearing process? Where? How much? Also, will such training be sufficient to enable them to cope with strong lawyer advocates? If lawyers they must be, are there enough of them available?

What other qualifications should hearing officers have? Is general legal or administrative experience sufficient, or must they have had experience with the substantive problems of the welfare agency? Should they be required to take examinations as a prerequisite to appointment? It might be noted that in the new Supplemental Security Income Program (SSI), under which the Department of Health, Education and Welfare has assumed the administration of the "adult" welfare programs of the states (Title XVI of the Social Security Act), a new corps of federal hearing officers are being employed and are required to take examinations designed to test not only their expertise but, through an interview process, their "judicial temperament."

Another major concern is the independence of the hearing officers. Should they have authority to make initial decisions, namely, those not subject to off-the-record changes by others in the system? Must they take budgetary constraints into consideration in arriving at decisions? To what extent should hearing officers deal with policy matters? The last question, like some of the others, confronts all administrative agencies that engage in adjudicative functions and goes to the most fundamental aspects of the role of an administrative adjudicative officer.

The Hearing System

Two factors pointed out by conference participants indicated that the hearing system is being overworked. Mr. Chauncey Alexander, representing the National Association of Social Workers, Washington, D.C., pointed out that some fifty percent of the claimants have legitimate claims. This, he said, is a "reflection on the administrative operations of the agency itself" rather than on the hearing system. What is important is to improve the performance of administrators and workers who are dealing with clients before they get to the problem of hearings, and thus substantially reduce the caseload. (It should be noted that other participants stated that the national average of legitimate claims was about 30 percent.)

The second point, made by Professor Jameson Doig of the Woodrow Wilson School at Princeton University, is one he identified as "incentive structures that are set up by agencies." He mentioned regulations referred to in the discussions which had to do with HEW's concern that state agencies may engage in overpayments to clients:

> Knowing that there will be penalties for overpayment, but nothing so significant for underpayment, uncertain cases will be decided negatively, that is, against the client. . . . A further result . . . is that the degree of systematic bias or incentive structure becomes known to those . . . who are involved in bringing legal action on behalf of clients. [This] is going to generate an increase in the number of fair hearings because of the clear perception . . . that a set of incentive structures set up which systematically insure that uncertain cases will be decided in one direction rather than another is going to lead to a set of individual fair hearings, burdening the system more, because of the desire to rebalance that bias in the . . . system.

The fair hearing process itself, moreover, has been subjected to increased pressures. The Supreme Court, in the landmark case of Goldberg v. Kelly,[4] which is dealt with in detail in Professor Baum's discussion, held that welfare termination adjudications are subject

xi

to the due process clause of the Constitution. The essential procedures include adequate and timely notice, the opportunity to retain counsel, the right to oral presentation, the right to confront and cross-examine adverse witnesses, impartial hearing officers, and a reasoned decision.

Professor Doig placed the problem in perspective:

What factors determine the need for formalized procedures in the relationship between staff and client? . . . It would seem clear that in some organizations . . . one does not need highly formalized procedures. Dan Baum referred in his paper to the Veterans Administration as an example in which there is a substantial degree of good will and a feeling of common goals between the staff member and the client. Insofar as that is true in the Veterans Administration or in unemployment compensation or as it once was in universities in the relationship between faculty and students, it's not essential to have such formal procedure set forth. Well, for those of us who have come through the last six or seven years in universities, we know that when that degree of good will—when the feeling of common goals, of empathy you might say—of mutual empathy and rapport breaks down, then there are going to be pressures, inevitable pressures to formalize procedures. . . . In the welfare field, it seems clear that in the United States that kind of good will between staff and client has broken down, if in fact it ever existed. The reasons why and the problems in the effort to control costs that generate some of that breakdown of good will, I think, have been discussed throughout this conference. One of the specific aspects of that, of course, is the development or the concern for the development of increasingly formalized procedures regarding the fair hearing process. Goldberg v. Kelly and then the much more detailed set of regulations set down by HEW generate a substantial burden or appear likely to generate a substantial burden in the processing of cases. This substantial burden occurs in part because there is not the good will and set of common goals that one might like between the agency members and the client.

Goldberg v. Kelly presents a formidable challenge to students of mass administrative justice. Can the multitudinous adjudications which come within its ambit, which is not limited to the welfare field

xii

but is already being applied in many others, be conducted within a judicial, due process framework? Will the adjudicative machinery be clogged? Is there some flexibility within this framework? The Supreme Court said there was, but did not explicate. Can simpler, equally satisfactory mechanisms be devised? Does Goldberg v. Kelly lock us into the adversary system in the adjudication of claims for the distribution by the government of funds, services, and goods? It might be noted in this connection that no nongovernmental activity is subject to such constraint, although there is some movement in that direction as in the development of rights of students and faculties, members of unions, and members of stock exchanges.

The right and opportunity to legal representation is a key element in the adversary system. Is it realistic to expect that such representation can be provided in mass administrative justice areas, either by the persons affected or by government subsidy? In the welfare area, in some instances, lay representatives have appeared on behalf of recipients, sometimes sponsored by nonprofit organizations. Is there any substantial promise in such a development?

A new and controversial mechanism introduced into the welfare system by recent federal regulations is the "local evidentiary hearing." Ronald A. Zumbrunn, Special Counsel to the Department of Health, Education and Welfare, explained this at the conference:

> The basic philosophy of the regs is to give flexibility and give options to the states or to the counties, depending on how the state is administered, to solve the problems that confront that county. It's a common sense approach and locking jurisdictions into certain hoops they have to jump through or certain very fixed requirements aimed at due process is not always due process, and, because of its impact on the entire class of recipients—and you have to look at both those who are before the fair hearing officer as well as those who may be waiting to get there and don't have aid pending.

What seems unclear in such a procedure is whether the local evidentiary hearing would be subject to Goldberg v. Kelly constraints. If they are not, then another hearing would be required which would appear to put additional strains on both the system and the recipient.

Checks on the Hearing Officer and the System

The most frequent check on the system and its officers discussed at the conference and the seminar was that of "quality control,"

xiii

or "quality assurance systems." For our purpose this would involve the institution of a regular system of statistical sampling and evaluation of the adjudication of claims for welfare benefits. It was maintained by some that to the extent that such systems are presently in operation they are designed simply to control costs. It was urged that they be recognized as "essential to the timely, accurate, and fair adjudication of claims of entitlement to benefits and compensation."[5] Such "positive caseload management" would include the following three connected operations:

> (1) the development of standards and methods for measuring the accuracy, timeliness and fairness of agency adjudications; (2) the continuous evaluation of agency adjudications with respect to those standards; and (3) the use of the information gathered in the course of evaluation as a basis for improving adjudicative performance.[6]

Such controls would undoubtedly be useful as an internal management mechanism for identifying causes underlying the finding that 30 to 50 percent of the adjudicative claims filed were legitimate. Unless it can be demonstrated that such an internal check can be made free from administrative manipulation, outside checks remain essential.

Judicial review, of course, is the primary check on administrative adjudications as to their legality, procedural fairness, and support by substantial evidence. Although this is an excellent check, it requires lawyers, preparation of formal documents such as notices of appeal and briefs, reproduction of the record, and the usual delays encountered in the appellate process. A minuscule number of welfare claims can go this route, because of lack of funds, lack of sophistication, and lack of available lawyers. Moreover, if many did, court calendars would be inundated.

Are there any other mechanisms available, or which could be made available, to provide an adequate check? This question pertains to many other areas of mass administrative justice. At present, the answer is that there are no other mechanisms generally in use at present and this is one of the great lacunae in modern administrative law.

It thus becomes the responsibility of the concerned community to find new ways of dealing with this problem. One real possibility would be in the adaptation of the "ombudsman" mechanism to the special area of welfare adjudication. Such an office would be established in addition to other remedies or rights of appeal, as an independent, impartial agency, empowered to investigate and criticize acts of agencies or administrators, in response to complaints by members of the public or on its own initiative, and to recommend changes toward the goals of safeguarding the rights of persons and promoting higher standards of competency, efficiency, and justice in the administration of law.[7]

Aside from the increasing number of ombudsmen and ombudsmen-like offices already established in many foreign nations, there has been some growth in the number of such offices in the United States within state and local governments, schools, colleges, correctional institutions, and mental health institutions. These have been created through both legislation and executive action.[8] An American Bar Association resolution adopted in 1969 lists twelve "essentials" for such an office, including authority to criticize all agencies and officials, independence from control by any other administrative officer, access to all relevant records, and discretionary power to determine what complaints to investigate and to determine what criticisms to make or to publicize.

It would seem that this type of office could be established in each state to function efficaciously as a check on welfare adjudications. It would act both on informal complaints by recipients and on its own initiative. It would not only seek to redress individual complaints but would also recommend administrative changes. Since it would have its own investigative staff, there would be a minimum of expense on the part of the complaining party. Certainly, where there is misunderstanding, such an office can perform a salutatory service. Also, the fact that there is such an overview could tend to improve administrative performance.

ROLE OF THE CENTER

The participants at both the conference and the seminar urged the Center for Administrative Justice to continue and enlarge upon its efforts in the field of welfare adjudication. The consensus was that, as an American Bar Association entity, and with its affiliation with a major university, it could function objectively in this area, a much needed attribute at this time. The chairman of one workshop summarized the general view of his group: "The Center, especially when seen in terms of its association with the American Bar, offers a rational neutrality in reviewing due process and fairness." It was urged to undertake a number of tasks, as follows:

Training Programs. The Center should develop a replicable adjudicator training program which could be offered on state, regional, and national levels. It should also provide programs for high-level administrators. Moreover, the training programs should be standardized, so that schools and agencies could use them as models. They should not be confined to a narrow view of the functions and procedures of adjudicators, but should expose trainees to basic due process principles and varying views of the social situation. The Center should prepare training materials, not only for adjudicators but also for caseworkers and technicians.

Models and Standards. The Center should develop models for state hearing systems and models for significant elements in the hearing process, such as a model notice. The Center should also develop standards for the entire system of review of decisions.

Hearing Officers. The Center should try to develop standards for the qualifications of adjudicators and standards for adjudicative practices. It is essential that provision be made for the maximum degree of independence for adjudicators to assure a fair hearing, yet responsive to agency policy. There is also a need to develop sensitivity in adjudicators to the capacity of the claimant to cope with the adjudicative process.

Research and Evaluation. The Center should attempt to develop techniques for conducting research in and evaluation of state hearing systems. It is important that mechanisms be developed to enable the systems to be evaluated on an ongoing basis.

Representation. The Center should explore the feasibility of and need for large-scale representation in the welfare hearing process. Much of the difficulty for claimants revolves around the meaning of notice and their access to resources that provide an opportunity to respond.

Conferences and Seminars. The Center should hold conferences and seminars where the various professions involved in welfare administration can meet to exchange ideas and experiences toward improving the processes of welfare administration.

These are large orders, and some are probably beyond the capabilities of the Center. However, as noted before, these concerns, although framed in terms of the needs in the welfare adjudication system, apply in many respects to other areas coming within the spectrum of mass administrative justice, and so there may be justification for their implementation.

NOTES

1. The quotations are taken from tapes and transcripts and thus may not present the author's views with precision.

2. American Bar Association Journal, 1974.

3. Ibid.

4. 397 U.S. 254, 1970.

5. Professor Jerry L. Mashaw, University of Virginia Law School, in a paper presented to the Administrative Conference of the United States, May 1973.

6. Ibid.

7. This statement is based upon an introductory provision of a "Model Ombudsman Statute for State Governments" prepared by the Yale Legislative Services.

8. In a recent contract between the City of New York and the Health Insurance Plan, provision is made for the establishment of an independent ombudsman's office, who will have wide powers to respond to ombudsmen's complaints. New York Times, February 1, 1974.

The Welfare Family and
Mass Administrative Justice

DETERMINANTS FOR FAIR ADMINISTRATION

The problem of providing fair hearings in the administration of welfare programs, particularly Aid to Families with Dependent Children, requires consideration of a complex of interacting factors. They affect massive numbers of people (and thus, mass administrative justice), require huge outlays of money, involve conflicting values and interests, and operate under a division of authority between the federal government, on the one hand, and the various state governments, on the other, which, because of differing policies, employ diverse and manipulative practices.

Some of the dimensions of the subject are indicated by the fact that in 1972 more than 13 million persons received maintenance assistance under the federal government's categorical aids program, at a cost of $10.5 billion. By far the largest category is Aid to Families with Dependent Children (AFDC), which includes about 10.5 million persons. The aid they receive is their primary source of support, and it amounted to $6.5 billion in 1972.

People and dollars are the basic elements in the perspective of welfare. It is around these two factors that all other considerations revolve. Values, rights or privileges, administrative responsibilities, and the type of fair hearing mechanisms relate to those basics. And it is clear that, despite attempts to redefine "gratuity" or "benefit" as the "new property," it is the government that determines how much money will be appropriated and spent. Such appropriation and spending can be increased, and also can be decreased without violating legal rights. The fair hearing aspect operates only toward ensuring fair treatment based upon whatever funds government has made available.

The question is then posed: To what extent do considerations other than due process affect the fair handling of welfare cases? It

1

may be posited that, to the extent to which the administrative apparatus
and the welfare recipients share the same goals, an environment for
fairness may exist. It can be argued that, the more diverse the goals,
the greater the possibility of unfairness. The problems, we hope,
can be illuminated by defining welfare and examining the pressures
on the apparatus for its administration.

Before doing this, however, a caveat must be sounded. There
are those who argue strongly that the quality of a hearing need have
absolutely no relationship to agency goals as such. It does not matter
that the agency and the claimant are in an adversary position; there
will still be a fair hearing. Such was the thrust of a letter written
to the author by Robert Best, former Chief Referee for the State of
California:

> I do not agree that the fair hearing is an arena where
> adverse interests and attitudes necessarily clash head-
> on. The purpose of the fair hearing is to elicit facts
> which describe a person's circumstances and then apply
> those facts in an objective manner to the laws and regu-
> lations governing the particular welfare program. In
> California, at least, the hearing officers and referees
> are encouraged to be highly objective and independent in
> their determination of the facts and the application of
> those facts to the laws and regulations. The "opposing
> interests" clash at a higher level, in the legislature or
> in the administrative proceedings associated with the
> adoption of state regulations where pitched battles
> between those who seek more for welfare recipients
> and who would give no more are staged. I cannot
> agree that it is fair to imply that this warring of op-
> posed interests passes down to the fair hearing function
> in welfare.

Best seems to be saying that California, the state that holds
the largest number of fair hearings, has opted for an objective fair
hearing system in adjudicatory matters. An independent body of
decision makers, rewarded only on the bases of their integrity and
competency, has been established to resolve individual disputes.
Facts are determined and then applied to the law. Values as to
claimant or welfare perception do not enter either in determining
facts or discovering the law applied to those facts. Best argues, in
summary, for a positivist view of law-finding. Whether his view is
correct might be better determined on the basis of the description
and analyses that follow, including the description of California's
fair hearing system.

MASS ADMINISTRATIVE JUSTICE: THE EXAMPLE
OF VETERANS' BENEFITS

The 1941 Attorney General's Report on Administrative Procedure touched on the problem of mass administrative justice. That report stated: "Initial informal decision is an essential device in disposing of large numbers of claims and license applications."[1] Formal proceedings simply were not deemed adequate to deal with the "vast number" of claims presented under the Railroad Retirement Act, the Social Security Act, and especially the claims handled by the Veterans Administration (VA), which then numbered more than 100,000 annually. A swift, simple, and fair informal process had to be developed to handle the great volume of issues. Indeed, this informal process, in the view of the 1941 Attorney General's Committee, took precedence over the admitted need to develop a thorough and impartial procedure for hearing those cases where the claimant and the government are unable to reach agreement. The committee particularly noted that in only 10 percent of the total claims submitted to the VA was there need for hearings before initial decision.

Each of the agencies mentioned by the committee, particularly the VA, had rather fully developed the informal infrastructure for decision making thought so essential. The claimant was assisted in the preparation and development of his claim by representatives of the agency accessible in the field. Special administrative units were available when specialized knowledge was needed for decision:

> In the Railroad Retirement Board and the Veterans Administration, for example, medical experts and occupational specialists are on hand to decide questions arising in the fields in which they are peculiarly proficient. Similarly, the Social Security Board has created subdivisions which deal with cases involving difficult or unusual problems. . . . Upon the basis of the information gathered by their staffs and submitted informally by the claimants, the agencies—often through field officers—make their initial decisions. In the vast majority of cases these decisions are accepted by the claimants. Only where they are not, are formal proceedings with witnesses and arguments and appeals to reviewing bodies invoked.[2]

The informal structure for decision making described and praised by the 1941 committee possessed certain characteristics: It was swift, simple, and fair. Those characteristics were achieved in no small measure because the public policy of the agencies and the goals of their staffs were in harmony with those of the claimants.

Certainly this remains true for many veterans even today. There exists a very close relationship between the VA and the veterans' organizations that represent most claimants.[3] So long as the veteran does not go counter to the goals of the VA and the veterans' organizations, help can be found. Yet, quite obviously, if the veteran goes counter to those goals, he may find reluctant assistance at best. The veteran's fair treatment may be dependent on individual compliance with organizational objectives.

The VA is set up on a state-by-state basis to facilitate interaction with veterans' organizations. The latter organizations frequently are housed in VA offices. These representatives can deal directly with the adjudicatory branch, thus bypassing VA contact personnel. And, finally, there is rather full access given to both files and initial decisions.[4] To indicate the size and importance of on-site institutional representatives, the American Legion maintains 17,000 service representatives throughout the nation.[5]

More important than the VA infrastructure for disposing of applications is that agency's effort to inform veterans of benefit programs in the first instance. It may be obvious, but it nevertheless must be stated, that there will be no application for benefits if the potential applicant is unaware of what might be his:

> The VA has a very elaborate outreach program at discharge points, hospitals and the veteran's place of residence. If the veteran wants to apply for benefits he apparently need merely reply affirmatively to any of the several entreaties that he will receive from the VA upon discharge. Special outreach programs are designed for persons with less than a high school education.[6]

The VA, the veterans' organizations, and the veteran often are in harmony in their articulated goals. To the extent that this is so, the veteran can expect not only objectivity but sympathy from both the VA and the veterans' organizations. Can the same be said of the welfare agency and the welfare claimant? Is there a melding of interest between the welfare agency and the welfare claimant? If the answer is affirmative, then an environment exists favorable to the creation of a mechanism that will not only reach out to inform recipients of welfare programs but also yield informal decisions swiftly, simply, and fairly. The agency could delegate to trusted staff and the welfare claimant could accept such delegation.

WELFARE DEFINED

In a very real sense, veterans' benefits can be categorized as a form of welfare, but they are not. A veteran's benefit is deemed earned through service to country. From the time of the Revolution, this perception was taken by the federal government. Handler and Goodstein vividly describe the difference in Wisconsin in the treatment of Civil War veterans and paupers:

> Immediately after the war, the state established a separate institution for children of deceased Wisconsin soldiers. This was the first state institution for orphans, and was an attempt to distinguish the Civil War orphans from other dependent children in order to avoid the pauper stigma. In the words of Governor Fairchild, "These children, to whom we owe so much, cannot be the objects of charity from the state. They are the beloved wards of the state, and when it provides for them a home and an education, it pays but little of the debt it owes them." Without this state intervention, these orphans could have been sent to various private orphanages, bound out to a "respectable" householder, or sent to the poorhouses. The movement to establish and continue this state orphanage received, of course, the strong support of Civil War veterans.
> The aging Civil War veterans caused the legislature to make a further distinction among the poor. Counties were authorized to levy taxes for the relief of "indigent union soldiers, sailors or marines, and the indigent wives and minor children of indigent or deceased veterans." Significantly, the statute required that this aid program be administered by a board of three commissioners, two of whom were required to be veterans. The purpose of this particular form of administration was to "separate the soldiers' relief from poor relief in the minds of the public and of the recipient, and because the officers who administer it are old soldiers and can understand and sympathize with the old soldiers better than civilians can." Civil War veterans and their families were not to be considered morally degenerate. In the words of the State Board of Charities, needy soldiers were not a "class of professional paupers, but are poor from misfortune".[7]

By contrast, welfare benefits, as such, did not become a subject of legislative concern to the federal government until 1935. Even then welfare was perceived as a scheme of social insurance; Title II of the Social Security Act dealt with "provisions relating to old age and survivors' insurance." Employees and employers both were to contribute to a social insurance scheme that had extremely broad coverage.

Frances Perkins and Rexford Tugwell, two close advisers to President Roosevelt, argued against employee contributions. The essence of their arguments was that those least able to pay would be funding the social insurance scheme. Some years later, after the Social Security Act was in effect, replying to another complainant, President Roosevelt said, "I guess you're right on the economics, but those taxes were never a problem of economics. They are politics all the way through. We put those payroll contributions there so as to give the contributors a legal, moral, and political right to collect their pensions and unemployment benefits. With those taxes in there, no damn politician can ever scrap my social security program."[8]

Old age and survivors' insurance was not to be viewed as a welfare benefit paid by the government to those in need. On the contrary, social security insurance is a pension paid for during an employee's working life. The federal government is important to this insurance scheme because it has declared as a matter of law that it shall exist; moreover, the federal government is in fact the insurer.

But Title II dealing with old age and survivors' insurance (and later disability insurance) was not the only title to the Social Security Act of 1935, although it surely was thought the most important not only in asserting a federal welfare role but also in terms of dollar expenditure.[9] In other titles, for the first time, the federal government came to the aid of the states, the traditional dispensers of welfare, by making grants of benefits to those in need. The Social Security Act defined those needs as categorical aids: aid to the blind (Title X); old age assistance (Title I); aid to families with dependent children (Title IV); aid to the permanently and totally disabled (Title XIV); and, most recently, medical assistance for the aged (Medicaid), a service linked to the categorical aids.

Until the late 1960s, thirty years after the enactment of the Social Security Act, it can be said that the federal government's role relating to categorical aids to many seemed largely that of providing monies to the states on a matching basis that ranged as high as 75-25—that is, the federal government would provide up to 75 cents of every dollar paid out by the states in the form of categorical aid. Other than definition of subject, there were no meaningful attempts by the federal government through the then Federal Security Agency, which later became part of the Department of Health, Education and Welfare, to control or provide direction to welfare programs. It was left to the states to determine individual need and the extent to which

6

that need would be funded. There was no compulsion on any state—as a matter of law—to fund fully individual need falling with a category in which the federal government provided assistance.

Yet within the federal agency, others have argued, there has been a sustained drive by such key civil servants as agency head Arthur J. Altmeyer; Jane Hoey, director of the old Bureau of Public Assistance; A. D. Smith, assistant general counsel of the Federal Security Agency; and Jack Tate. As one close observer has stated:

> They furnished leadership which . . . gave the first real meaning to the concept that an individual does have equal protection and due process rights in relation to his claim for public assistance. In the implementation of the new program of Federal grants, they fought long, hard, and successfully to keep partisan political influence out of the decision making process of the welfare programs. They felt it essential to avoid a spoils system in the employment of State and local personnel, so they undertook a difficult battle to obtain a requirement in the 1939 amendments that State welfare plans as a condition of getting Federal assistance must employ personnel under a merit system which would be in compliance with Federal personnel standards. Having won the legislative victory, they struggled in innumerable situation with States for the enforcement of proper policies.
> It is true that only a small number of conformity hearings for the withdrawal of Federal grants were held during these years. This overlooks, however, both the significance of the hearings which were held and the fact that at that time the statute did not permit the withdrawal of funds for only that part of the plan which failed to conform. A finding of nonconformity would require a withdrawal of all funds to the State for the category of the program involved. As with a nuclear bomb, this weapon packed such a potential wallop that it was rarely used, but did produce negotiations which produced meaningful results. There were innumerable instances of showdowns with State which . . . a study would show produced important broad policy results protective of individual rights under such important Federal requirements as State-wide effect of the plan, consideration of income and resources in determining the amount of the assistance, provision of opportunity for fair hearing, merit system standards, etc. One instructive example of enforcement is the confirmity hearing that was held in the late 1940's concerning the

7

refusal of Arizona and New Mexico to give full assistance
rights to Indians. There was no specific provision in the
Act which authorized the withdrawal of Federal funds in
such a situation. Among other things, the Federal action
was based upon a theory that a Federal grant contained
an implicit condition that the State use it in accordance
with equal protection concepts. This is pretty well established now, but [there was] no other Federal grant program which was so bold as to make such a contention until many years thereafter. In fact, such a concept was not
generally recognized elsewhere until after enactment of
Title VI of the Civil Rights Act of 1964 which is a statutory recognition of the concept. . . . [A] good case can be
made that Mr. Smith's thinking of 20 years back played a
large part in the establishment of the currently accepted
judicial views on the constitutional protection which at-
taches to the administration of public grant programs.[10]

The point is that for many years, and until very recently, welfare
administration—unlike old age, survivors', and disability insurance—
was within the exclusive domain of the states. Indeed, even now (more
will be said of this later) welfare remains an area subject to the influence of much state law and practice. For welfare recipients the
Social Security Act of 1935 announced no clear new substantive policy;
no obviously new social contract was created vesting a "property
right" to benefits in the welfare recipients as distinguised from Title
II Social Security benefits. Quite the contrary is true. The concept
of property as contrasted to gratuity was carried forward. Because
employees paid for their social insurance, they acquired, if not a de
jure, at least a de facto property interest in that insurance. Moreover,
the very nomenclature of "categorical aids" tended to preserve the
historic basis for categorizing deserving poor apart from those who
were a drain on society. Indeed, it was an ongoing struggle for the
Federal Security Agency to stretch the new federal law by interpretation to provide individual rights that were not clearly stated in federal
statute.

In a very real sense, it can be argued that the Social Security
Act carried forward the concepts of biological determinism and social
Darwinism, to wit: Pauperism is a disease with little hope for re-
covery because it is rooted in heredity. Those who are poor stand
in great danger of contracting the disease. Still, for a liberal society
it may be well to aid in sifting out the "deserving poor" from those
doomed to pauperism. Who are the deserving poor? They are those
whom fate has marked: the blind, the aged, the abandoned mothers
with small children at home—the "categorical aids" of the Social

Security Act of 1935. Those so marked were not to be treated as paupers. They were not to be compelled even as early as 1850 to obtain certificates of pauperism as a condition for the grant of aid. This was especially true of the blind and the aged.

Dependent children, like the blind and the aged, were characterized as deserving poor. They were different from the general mass of the poor; they were capable of being helped. Yet in saying this let there be no doubt that even the deserving poor were considered objects of welfare in the sense of gratuities flowing from the states. They possessed no right to call upon the resources of the states—they only possessed the right, once qualified, to share in such resources as the states might appropriate.

Aid to dependent children came several years after aid to the blind and aged. It came as a result of the Child-Saving movement of the latter half of the nineteenth century. The thrust of that movement was to save the predelinquent and delinquent child by placing that person in an institutional "family" setting. This meant the establishment of a juvenile court that was not a court but a familial structure for long-term correction. It meant the establishment of reformatories rather than prisons as places to send children. The reformatories ideally would be located in rural areas, and physically would be cottages rather than massive stone buildings. The conceptual base of the Child-Savers seemed to be that children were capable of being saved, of redemption, for their character was not yet molded.

The first aid to dependent children's statute (ADC) was that of Illinois in 1911. That statute was an amendment to the state's Juvenile Court Act.[11] The Illinois act, and those that followed, it has been suggested, flowed from the 1909 White House Conference on the Care of Dependent Children, which as a major conclusion stated:

> Home life is the highest and finest product of civilization. It is the great molding force of mind and of character. Children should not be deprived of it except for urgent and compelling reasons. Children of parents of worthy character, suffering from temporary misfortune and children of reasonably efficient and deserving mothers who are without the support of the normal breadwinner, should, as a rule, be kept with their parents, such aid being given as may be necessary to maintain suitable homes for the rearing of the children. This aid should be given by such methods and from such sources as may be determined by the general relief policy of each community, preferably in the form of private charity, rather than of public relief. Except in unusual circumstances, the home should not be broken up for reasons of poverty, but only for considerations of inefficiency or immorality.[12]

President Theodore Roosevelt added his own emphasis to this conclusion in transmitting the text of the conference report. He called attention to the number of dependent children in institutions and then said:

> Each of these children represents either a potential addition to the production capacity and the enlightened citizenship of the nation, or, if allowed to suffer from neglect, a potential addition to the destructive forces of the community. The ranks of the criminals and other enemies of society are recruited in an altogether undue proportion from children bereft of their natural homes and left without sufficient care.[13]

Following the 1911 conference, within the next biennium, twenty states enacted ADC legislation. The structure of that legislation generally followed the Illinois mold:

1. The law was drafted as an amendment to the juvenile court act.
2. The child was to be found dependent; that is, the child must be found "neglected, destitute, abandoned, homeless, or in any manner dependent upon the public for support, or whose parents, or person occupying the position of a parent, for any reason are unable without aid, properly to maintain, bring up or educate such child."[14]
3. It must be in the best interest of the child to remain within the family unit. The determination of this matter was that of the court (operating in a juvenile court-type environment).
4. The court could award such sum as it deemed sufficient to maintain the child. That sum, however, could not exceed the amount allowed by legislation plus a maximum additional allowance for special needs such as medical services.
5. The individual, as such, was not the only one who could call upon the court for relief. The task was also assigned to the county or local townships, which could make an initial determination that a case for grant of relief was stated, and then petition on the child's behalf to the court. Indeed, the statute was drafted in such a way as to place the burden on the county or township first and the individual second.

THE SOCIAL SECURITY ACT OF 1935:
ITS STRUCTURE

The point was made in the preceding section that the Social Security Act of 1935, on its face and for a period of thirty years, basically constituted a federal funding mechanism that left the states substantially free to do as they would with categorical aids. A word of explanation is needed; the legislative history of the Social Security Act as well as its basic structure touching upon categorical aids should be elaborated.

The categorical aids provision of the act became an experiment in "cooperative federalism." To repeat and emphasize, categorical aids provide financing on a matching basis under programs that are administered by the states. (This frequently means the states hold a supervisory role for programs are administered by counties or cities.) States desiring to take advantage of the federal matching funds are required to submit an Aid to Families with Dependent Children (AFDC) plan for the approvol of the Secretary of the Department of Health, Education and Welfare (HEW).[15] The plan must conform to several requirements of the act, as well as such regulations as the secretary might promulgate to fulfill the purposes of the act.[16]

Unless HEW approves the plan, federal funds will not be available for its implementation. Moreover, HEW may terminate federal payments in whole or in part if there is a failure to comply with any provision required to be a part of the plan as a result of federal law.[17] (It should be noted that the history of HEW and the Social Security Administration does not show many state conformity hearings.)[18]

State plans are to conform to federal statutory goals. One of those early statutory goals required that "aid to families with dependent children . . . shall be furnished with reasonable promptness to all eligible individuals."[19] The act defines a dependent child as one who has been deprived of parental support or care by reason of a parent's death, continued absence, or incapacity.[20] "In combination, these two provisions of the Act clearly require participating States to furnish aid to families with children who have a parent absent from home, if such families are in other respects eligible."[21]

Federal law is designed to aid the dependent child; that seems to be its clear thrust. Yet in 1935 there was little doubt that the states, in the enactment and implementation of their AFDC statutes, were also concerned with the morality of the mother. If the mother was found immoral, if children were conceived out of wedlock, if a man not the child's father cohabited with the mother, then the child was not deemed deserving of aid. "In this social context it is not surprising that both the House and Senate Committee Reports on the Social Security Act of 1935 indicate that States participating in AFDC were free to impose eligibility requirements relating to the 'moral character' of applicants."[22] During the years following 1935 many states kept and enlarged AFDC provisions denying aid to children not living in "suitable homes."[23]

In the 1940s suitable home provisions came under increasing attack:

Critics argued, for example, that such disqualification
provisions undermined a mother's confidence and authority, thereby promoting continued dependency; that they
forced destitute mothers into increased immorality as a
means of earning money; that they were habitually used
to disguise systematic racial discrimination; and that
they senselessly punished impoverished children on the
basis of their mothers' behavior, while inconsistently per-
mitting them to remain in the alleged unsuitable homes.[24]

In 1945 the Federal Security Agency, predecessor of HEW,
urged the states to abolish the suitable home requirements. The following ten years found 15 states willing to accept and act upon that
argument.
        The 1950s, however, as we shall discuss more fully, saw state
appropriations for AFDC expand significantly. With that expansion
of budget came a corresponding desire to cut back on the undeserving,
and more particularly, the disqualification of illegitimate children.[25]
Again the federal government reacted strongly; illegitimacy does not
have much to do with a child's need; moreover, the child was not
responsible for the act of illegitimacy.
        In 1960 Louisiana enacted legislation imposing as a condition
precedent for AFDC eligibility that the dependent child's home be
suitable. In this regard, any home in which an illegitimate child had
been born subsequent to the receipt of public assistance was to be
considered unsuitable.[26]
        Secretary Fleming of HEW, in the exercise of his rule-making
power, issued what became known as the Fleming Ruling, which stated
that as of July 1, 1961:

        A State plan . . . may not impose an eligibility condition
        that would deny assistance with respect to a needy child
        on the basis that home conditions in which the child lives
        are unsuitable, while the child continues to reside in the
        home. Assistance will therefore be continued during the
        time efforts are being made to improve the home or to
        make arrangements for the child elsewhere.[27]

Congress quickly approved the Fleming Ruling while extending until
September 1, 1962, the time for state compliance.[28]
        There have been a number of reasons for culling out and ex-
panding upon the example of the illegitimate child:
        1. It tends to demonstrate the potential role for federal action;
           it allows a line to be drawn between the states' legitimate
           interests and those of the federal government in providing
           aid to dependent children as such.

12

2. It indicates the area of administrative discretion available to the secretary of HEW to resolve issues in dispute; that is to say, the Louisiana legislation relating to illegitimate children might have been challenged in the courts either as being outside that permitted by the Social Security Act or as a constitutional matter (i.e., the denial of equal protection of the laws). The secretary, however, forestalled such action, and his ruling was later enforced by Congress.
3. The power potential of the secretary is subject to contraction as well as expansion. It is true that the secretary's ruling enforced recipient rights. By the same token, the secretary's nonaction for a period of more than a decade denied those rights. The point is simply that power need not always be expanded or used on behalf of recipients. Power is also subject to nonuse, to contraction.

NOTES

1. Attorney General's Committee on Administrative Procedure, "Administrative Procedure in Government Agencies," Sen. Doc. No. 8, 77th Cong., 1st Sess. (1941), reprinted by the University Press of Virginia 38 (1968).

2. Id., at 38-39.

3. M. Gilhooley, "Veterans Administration Disability Procedures," Staff Report for the Committee on Grant and Benefit Programs, Administrative Conference of the United States, Mar. 8, 1972, (mimeo.), at 22.

4. J. Mashaw, Consultant to the Committee on Grant and Benefit Programs, Administrative Conference of the United States, "Interim Report: Representation and Quality Control in the Adjudication of Claims for Disability Benefits," Nov. 3, 1972 (mimeo.), at 6.

5. Id., at 8.

6. Id., at 7.

7. See J. Handler and A. Goodstein, "The Legislative Development of Public Assistance," 1968 Wis. L. Rev. 414, 421-22.

8. A. Schlesinger, Jr., the Age of Roosevelt: The Coming of the New Deal (Boston: Houghton Mifflin, 1959), at 308-9.

9. Id., at 309. It was the interim funding of those ready for retirement that constituted the major dollar outlay.

10. Welfare Law, Center on Social Welfare Policy and Law, 1972 at IX-89: "HEW enforcement of its regulations, which has been notoriously lax in recent years, has, due to welfare rights and legal services pressure, been somewhat more effective in the area of fair hearings." HEW use, however, of "pre-prints," that is, checklist

forms for determining compliance by the states, is not conducive to effective compliance. See also, R. Scott, "The Regulation and Administration of the Welfare Hearing Process—The Need for Administrative Responsibility, 11 Wm. & Mary L. Rev. 291, 351 (1969). The lengthy quotation in the text comes from a letter written by Edwin Yourman, Assistant General Counsel-Social Security, HEW, to Professor Baum, May 22, 1973. His views were endorsed by Alanson S. Willcox, former General Counsel, HEW; letter from Willcox to Professor Baum June 9, 1973. See also, Note, "Welfare's Condition X," 76 Yale L.J. 1222 (1967).

11. Ch. 23, §175 (1911) Ill. Laws 126.

12. Proceedings of the Conference on the Care of Dependent Children, S. Doc. No. 721, 60th Cong., 2d Sess. 9, 10 (1909), cited in note 7 supra, at 429, note 66.

13. Id., at 6.

14. See, for example, Ch. 669, §2 (1913) Wis. Laws. 925.

15. 42 U.S.C. §§601-04. See, however, text at note 10 supra.

16. 42 U.S.C. §602.

17. 42 U.S.C. §601, 602(a).

18. See 42 U.S.C. §§604, 1204, 1354, 1384, 1396(c). States called to task for noncompliance must be afforded a hearing. Between 1936 and 1969 only 19 such hearings were called. From 1969 to 1971 additional hearings were called involving Arizona, California, Connecticut, Indiana, Missouri, and Nebraska. No conformity hearings have been called since 1971. 3 Welfare Law, Center on Social Welfare Policy and Law, 1972, at IX-425. See, however, text at note 10 supra.

19. 42 U.S.C. §602(a)(10).

20. 42 U.S.C. §606(a).

21. King v. Smith, 392 U.S. 309, 317 (1968).

22. Id., at 321.

23. Id.

24. Id., at 321-22.

25. See J. Handler and E. Hollingsworth, "Reforming Welfare: The Constraints of the Bureaucracy and The Clients," 118 U. Pa. L. Rev. 1167-69 (1970).

26. La. Acts No. 251 (1960).

27. State Letter No. 452, Bureau of Public Assistance, Social Security Administration, HEW.

28. 75 Stat. 77, as amended, 42 U.S.C. §604(b).

2

**FEDERAL ADMINISTRATIVE
DISCRETION AND
FAIR HEARINGS**

THE SOCIAL SECURITY ACT: FAIR HEARINGS

The generalizations made concerning the illegitimate child surface rather clearly in the fair hearing procedures under the Social Security Act:

1. The Constitution, through the due process clause, and the Social Security Act, provides bases for a federal welfare role. The states are not free to determine as they will the grant of categorical aid benefits.
2. The Constitution sets the bare minimum required for a fair hearing. As we shall see, the statute allows the secretary of HEW substantial discretion to expand upon the constitutional minimum.
3. The secretary has the same power to maintain the constitutional minimum. Indeed, through nonenforcement of minimum criteria, the secretary, in effect, could lower the constitutionally declared standards.

There has been an ebb and flow to fair hearing requirements by the Social Security Administration. The Social Security Act requires: "A state plan . . . must . . . provide for granting an opportunity for a fair hearing before the state agency to any individual whose claim for [categorical aid under the plan] is denied or not acted upon with reasonable promptness."[1] Until July 1970 HEW construed the statutory proviso to mean that aid could be terminated first and a fair hearing—that is, a formal, on-the-record hearing—held second.[2]

For New York City an "informal" procedure for claims adjudication prior to cutoff was evolved as a matter of formal policy. A caseworker with doubts about a person's continued eligibility was first to have a discussion with the recipient. Following that discussion, if the doubts were not resolved, termination or modification could be recommended by the caseworker to the supervisor. If the supervisor agreed with the caseworker, a letter was sent notifying the recipient of the proposed termination of aid, but allowing seven days for a review petition to a higher agency official together with supporting written submissions. If the reviewing official affirmed the termination, aid was stopped immediately and the recipient was informed of a right to a "post-determination" fair hearing. Missing in New York City's "informal" procedure were the right to personal appearance before the reviewing official, oral presentation of evidence, and confrontation and cross-examination of adverse witnesses. In sum, procedural due process was missing.

In Goldberg v. Kelly the Supreme Court was faced with the narrow but important question of whether the due process clause requires that the recipient be afforded an evidentiary hearing before the termination of benefits.[3] For thirty years that question, as a matter of administrative practice had been answered in the negative by the Social Security Administration. In 1970 the Supreme Court held otherwise, in sharp, unequivocal language:

> But we agree with the District Court that when welfare
> is discontinued, only a pre-termination evidentiary hear-
> ing provides the recipient with procedural due process.
> Cf. Sniadach v. Family Finance Corp., 395 U. S. 337 (1969).
> For qualified recipients, welfare provides the means to
> obtain essential food, clothing, housing, and medical care.
> Cf. Nash v. Florida Industrial Commission, 389 U.S. 235,
> 239 (1967). Thus the crucial factor in this context—a
> factor not present in the case of the blacklisted govern-
> ment contractor, the discharged government employee,
> the taxpayer denied a tax exemption, or virtually anyone
> else whose governmental entitlements are ended—is that
> termination of aid pending resolution of a controversy
> over eligibility may deprive an eligible recipient of the
> very means by which to live while he waits. Since he
> lacks independent resources, his situation becomes
> immediately desperate. His need to concentrate upon
> finding the means for daily subsistence, in turn, ad-
> versely affects his ability to seek redress from the
> welfare bureaucracy.
>
> Moreover, important governmental interests are
> promoted by affording recipients a pre-termination
> evidentiary hearing. From its founding the Nation's basic
> commitment has been to foster the dignity and well-being
> of all persons within its borders. We have come to rec-
> ognize that forces not within the control of the poor con-
> tribute to their poverty. This perception, against the

16

background of our traditions, has significantly influenced the development of the contemporary public assistance system. Welfare, by meeting the basic demands of subsistence, can help bring within the reach of the poor the same opportunities that are available to others to participate meaningfully in the life of the community. At the same time, welfare guards against the societal malaise that may flow from a widespread sense of unjustified frustration and insecurity. Public assistance, then, is not mere charity, but a means to "promote the general Welfare, and secure the Blessings of Liberty to ourselves and our Posterity." The same governmental interests that counsel the provision of welfare, counsel as well its uninterrupted provision to those eligible to receive it; pre-termination evidentiary hearings are indispensable to that end.[4]

Fiscal considerations were not deemed to outweigh individual need. It was not that the Court denied the legitimacy of such considerations. It was simply that the Court felt that innovation and flexibility might allow the state to meet its fiscal obligations and, at the same time, serve the interest of the individual dependent on welfare.

The Court, moreover, was rather precise in listing the defects of the New York City procedure. This the Court did while at the same time noting that the hearing need not be given a formal adjudicatory posture. Among the defects the Court noted was the failure to allow the recipient to appear personally, face, and cross-examine adverse witnesses. The Court seemed doubtful that welfare recipients could be expected to reply to charges in writing or secondhand through a caseworker:

> Written submissions are an unrealistic option for most recipients, who lack the educational attainment necessary to write effectively and who cannot obtain professional assistance. Moreover, written submissions do not afford the flexibility of oral presentations; they do not permit the recipient to mold his argument to the issues the decision maker appears to regard as important. Particularly where credibility and veracity are at issue, as they must be in many termination proceedings, written submissions are a wholly unsatisfactory basis for decision. The secondhand presentation to the decision maker by the caseworker has its own deficiencies; since the caseworker usually gathers the facts upon which the charge

of ineligibility rests, the presentation of the recipient's side of the controversy cannot safely be left to him. Therefore a recipient must be allowed to state his position orally. Informal procedures will suffice; in this context due process does not require a particular order of proof or mode of offering evidence.[5]

For welfare recipients, a class of people who are often unable to express themselves clearly, it was all the more important that they be afforded the right of counsel. Through an attorney the recipient might better delineate issues and marshal facts in an orderly manner.[6]

The rights that the Court laid down in this landmark case would have little meaning, however, if the agency decision maker did not rule exclusively from a base of law and the evidence adduced at the hearing:

> To demonstrate compliance with this elementary requirement, the decision maker should state the reasons for his determination and indicate the evidence he ruled on . . . though his statement need not amount to a full opinion or even formal findings of fact and conclusions of law. And, of course, an impartial decision maker is essential. . . . We agree with the District Court that prior involvement in some aspects of a case will not necessarily bar a welfare official from acting as a decision maker. He should not, however, have participated in making the decision under review.[7]

Just before the Court's enunciation of due process principles in Goldberg v. Kelly, a revised set of fair hearing rules was proposed by HEW.[8] Indeed, the Court noted this fact in its opinion, but it nevertheless preferred to test and weigh the constitutional question against state practice.[9]

As finally promulgated, the regulations of HEW were comprehensive in their substantive terms.[10] They were given definition in fair hearing guides published by the Assistance Payments Administration of the Social and Rehabilitation Service. (The regulations and the guides are reproduced in Appendix A.) They were designed to cover all categorical aid programs, not merely AFDC.[11] It can be safely stated that the regulations went beyond the constitutional minima of Goldberg v. Kelly. Key to the new regulations was the requirement that aid could not be discontinued until after the state fair hearing decision, if it involved an issue of fact or judgment.[12] It was this key restriction, coupled with advance notice requirements, that placed real and new responsibilities on several states.

The end result favors the recipient, who maintains status and compensation. Yet it must be noted that by its terms Goldberg v. Kelly does not preclude the possibility of local evidentiary hearings conducted by caseworkers who have nothing to do with prior review of the matter in controversy.[13] Indeed, in 1973 HEW seized upon the Supreme Court opportunity for local evidentiary hearings in a revision of its rules, which are discussed in Chapter 4 of this book.

State hearings required by statute could be of an appellate nature. In its regulations, HEW opted for a stricter standard than that imposed by the Supreme Court interpreting the due process clause. That standard was reinforced by another: With only very narrowly drawn exceptions, any agency proposing to terminate, reduce, or suspend assistance is to give mailed notice of the pending action at least 15 days prior to the time of the anticipated action.[14] In passing, it is noted that the 15-day notice also includes the opportunity for a conference, informal discussion, full disclosure of the file, and possible compromise—with or without consent. The conference is not intended as a substitute for the state fair hearing.

The overall substantive effect of HEW regulations was to allow an initially determined ineligible recipient to be carried on the rolls for a period of at least 75 days. For the states, as we shall see, the dollar cost is quite substantial. For the recipient, there is the security of continued benefits until after the state fair hearings. In this regard, however, the regulations protect only existing benefits. They are not addressed to (1) application for the initial grant of benefits or to (2) the denial of claims for increased benefits flowing from changes in circumstances. As to both (1) and (2), the claimant will be compelled to await the outcome of the fair hearing decision. If the hearing decision is favorable to the claimant or if the agency decides in favor of the claimant prior to hearing, corrective payments, retroactive to the date of entitlement as provided in the state plan, or to the date of incorrect action, must be made.[15]

Strong emphasis has been placed on the welfare benefit status in a consideration of HEW regulations. Indeed, it was just such a consideration that played no small part in the Court's disposition of Goldberg v. Kelly. There the Court felt somewhat constrained to view the effect of termination of benefits prior to hearing as potentially devastating to the recipient. HEW regulations protect the existing benefits, assuring the states as they do so that the federal government will continue to provide its share of supporting funds for those fair hearing cases where the recipient is found ineligible for the claimed benefit. This is only mildly comforting to the states, which are still out of pocket for monies paid to ineligible applicants. Moreover, in a real sense, these are not recoverable monies by the very nature of the claimants' circumstances.

From the states' view, money cost is a primary consideration in their willingness to accept a given system for the distribution of justice. The money cost of HEW's regulations adopted after Goldberg v. Kelly was alleged to be high. Resistance was encountered from the states, and as late as May 1973 Arizona and North Carolina refused to comply fully.[16] A rather sharp correlation can be found between a state's willingness to accept the full panoply of procedural due process and lower money cost. This is said even though Pennsylvania and Maryland, state-supervised, locally administered jurisdictions, not only have been in compliance with the HEW regulations but seem, on the whole, content with them. An official from Maryland said: "Sure we're content now. The regulations are law and we are trying to make them work. In my personal, not official view, it cannot be demonstrated that adequate hearings at a local level are more efficient or less costly than adequate hearings at a state level. Therefore, I believe that the issue is not a real one, at least in the form it is usually put, and there would not be much pressure in this state to change the present, generally satisfactory system of fair hearings."

HEW's post-Goldberg rules, of course, went beyond money protection in terms of advance notice and fair hearing. They embraced the points raised by Goldberg v. Kelly, namely, the right to representation by friend or counsel; the right to individual hearings even where the issue is common to a group; no denial or dismissal of a hearing request except where it has been withdrawn in writing by the claimant or abandoned; the right to hearings at times and places convenient to the claimant; the right to bring witnesses and to examine in full relevant government files used at the hearing; the right to "advance any arguments without undue interference"; the right to question or refute any testimony or evidence, including opportunity to confront and cross-examine adverse witnesses.

Detailed rules are also laid down for decision making. Decisions must be made within 60 days following the date of request for a fair hearing, except where the claimant asks for delay. The decision is to be made on the basis of the record, which includes and is limited to that reserved in evidence at the fair hearing. State fair hearing decisions must not only specify the reasons for the ruling but also identify the supporting evidence. (An examination of some New York decisions indicates only the most limited development of rationale and fact finding.) No person who participated in the local decision being appealed will take part in the final administrative decision. The state is responsible for the faithful carrying out of all decisions. Toward that end, the state is to develop and maintain at least a summary reporting system of all fair hearing decisions. (Maryland has made an attempt to prepare such summaries.)

The regulations have been held valid. Speaking for the Second Circuit in Almenares v Wyman, Chief Judge Friendly said:

> When we come at long last to the State's attack upon the validity of the HEW regulation, we join the district judge in finding it unimpressive. The State's general position is that HEW has no legitimate concern with the distribution of functions between the State and its subdivision in the administration of federally assisted programs so long as the right results are achieved. More specifically, the State cites 42 U.S.C. § 602 (a) which provides that "A State plan for aid and services to needy families with children must . . . (3) either provide for the establishment or designation of a single State agency to administer the plan, or provide for the establishment or designation of a single State agency to supervise the administration of the plan," and claims that the requirement for a State hearing before any adverse action deprives the State of the benefit of the latter option. But it is surely consistent with § 602 (a) (3) for HEW, under the broad rule-making authority accorded by 42 U.S.C. § 1302, to determine that State supervision must include the conduct of hearings prior to adverse action. This is especially so in light of § 602 (a) (4) which requires a State plan to "provide for granting an opportunity for a fair hearing before the State agency to any individual whose claim for aid to families with dependent children is denied or is not acted upon with reasonable promptness." It was competent for HEW to determine that the objectives of the federally assisted programs could be better attained by a single state hearing prior to the taking of action rather than having such a hearing conducted by a subdivision of the state subject to review in a state hearing after action had been taken.[17]

Individuals and representative groups have successfully sought their enforcement, calling upon the powers of the courts. The Supreme Court, in a per curiam opinion following Goldberg v. Kelly, seemed to indicate rather clearly that different HEW regulations as applied to the Old Age, Survivors, and Disability Insurance program (OASDI) should be allowed to operate, that they preclude the need to consider constitutional arguments of due process.[18] Indeed, in that regard, the view of the Court seemed to reflect the chief justice's dissent in Wheeler v. Montgomery,[19] a companion case to Goldberg. There the chief justice noted that the HEW fair hearing regulations for public assistance go far beyond the constitutional minima laid down by the Court: "Against this background I am baffled as to why we should engage in 'legislating' via constitutional fiat when an apparently reasonable result has been accomplished administratively."[20] Moreover, the chief justice continued:

> I can share the impatience of all who seek instant solutions; there is a great temptation in this area to frame remedies that seem fair and can be mandated forthwith as against administrative or congressional action that calls for careful and extended study that is thought too slow. But, however cumbersome or glacial, this is the procedure the Constitution contemplated.
>   I would not suggest that the procedures of administering the Nation's complex welfare programs are beyond the reach of courts, but I would wait until more is known about the problems before fashioning solutions in the rigidity of a constitutional holding.
>   By allowing the administrators to deal with these problems we leave room for adjustments if, for example, it is found that a particular gearing process is too costly. The history of the complexity of the administrative process followed by judicial review as we have seen it for the past 30 years should suggest the possibility that new layers of procedural protection may become an intolerable drain on the very funds earmarked for food, clothing and other living essentials.[21]

HEW fair hearing regulations were treated by many as if they were fixed rules, as if they had the durability of a Supreme Court constitutional holding. In fact, quite the contrary was true. Those regulations came under immediate attack from many states, including New York and California, and after less than two years of operation the regulations were substantially modified. The key to the rationale for modification is money cost—both to the federal government and to the states. That issue will be considered below. The essence of this discussion of HEW fair hearing procedures has simply been to indicate that administrative policy is subject to change, and that change is not necessarily determined on the basis of an evidentiary record.

THE FEDERAL BUDGET, AFDC,
AND FAIR HEARINGS

The federal budget proposals for fiscal 1974 provided a catalyst for many states to intensify their opposition to HEW's fair hearing regulations. In the budget the President proposed to eliminate federal funding of ineligible AFDC claimants. That is, as a result of quality

22

control checks involving statistical sampling, those found to be receiving AFDC payments improperly were to be discounted in the provision of matching funds to the states. Federal funding, however, would continue in contested cases pending completion of state fair hearings. The projected savings to the federal government for fiscal 1974 were estimated at about $456 million. These savings were based on quality controls that in the past showed a national error rate of about 5 to 6 percent. Although the language of the budget for fiscal year 1974 is not entirely clear, discussions within HEW have developed the thrust of the budget proposal concerning cutbacks to ineligibles:

> The estimates for maintenance assistance reflect transfer of the adult categories of maintenance assistance to Federal administration effective January 1, 1974. This reduces the 1974 costs under the appropriation by about $1.1 billion.
>
> The estimates for maintenance assistance for 1972 and 1973 have been adjusted to show the costs of the intermediate care facilities program in the medical assistance totals.
>
> New Federal initiatives are proposed in 1973 and 1974 to strengthen the Federal role in management of this program, focusing on aid to families with dependent children. This effort will save $128 million in 1973 and a total of $750 million in 1974. The 1974 savings include $158 million to result from legislation which will be proposed.[22]

Like the states, the President evidenced a real concern over the enormous growth in AFDC claimants. From 1935 to 1950 total AFDC expenditures did not exceed $500 million. "The total doubled between 1950 and 1960. From 1960 to 1967, another one billion in expenditures was added."[23] In 1972 there were 10.5 million recipients of AFDC for a total dollar outlay of $6.5 billion. In 1973 there was about a 10 percent increase and 11,846,000 recipients received AFDC for a total cost of $7.1 billion. A projected further increase for 1974 is given: There will be an estimated 12.5 million recipients of AFDC for a total cost of $7.74 billion (see Tables 1 and 2).

The presidential cut does not require the approval of Congress, or at least that seems to be the view of the Executive. The Social and Rehabilitation Service of HEW, charged with much of the responsibility for categorical aids, and AFDC especially, announced proposed rules on December 5, 1972, that would carry forward the budget proposals.[24] Additional time for comment was granted and proposed implementation of the proposed rule was set for April 1, 1973, only to be postponed again.[25]

TABLE 1

Maintenance Assistance Program Costs
(in thousands of dollars)

	1972	1973*	1974*
Old age assistance	1,843,424	1,844,596	900,514
Aid to the blind	98,567	106,961	54,190
Aid to the permanently and totally disabled	1,240,146	1,489,096	847,071
Aid to families with dependent children	6,553,599	7,196,131	7,742,859
Emergency assistance	42,815	71,595	55,785
State and local administration	752,252	932,719	906,199
Total: federal, state, and local	10,530,803	11,641,098	10,506,618
Federal share	5,945,907	6,498,006	5,543,541

Source: Appendix to the Budget for Fiscal Year 1974.

TABLE 2

Maintenance Assistance Recipient Caseload

	Average Monthly Number		
	1972	1973	1974*
Old age assistance	2,021,795	2,008,823	2,018,938
Aid to the blind	79,437	81,305	83,469
Aid to the permanently and totally disabled	1,047,440	1,179,936	1,353,430
Aid to families with dependent children	10,539,972	11,465,838	12,534,231
Emergency assistance	23,244	41,267	33,399
Total	13,711,888	14,777,169	16,023,467

Source: Appendix to the Budget for Fiscal Year 1974.

*Cost reductions in 1973 and 1974 result from management initiatives to be placed in effect and from the transfer of the adult categories to the Social Security Administration effective January 1, 1974. Caseload estimates have not been reduced correspondingly. In 1974 caseload totals for the aged, blind, and disabled are the monthly averages for July through December 1973.

In a press release of December 4, 1972, Secretary Richardson elaborated on the rationale for the change. The full national sub-sample of data from quality control systems of the states, then available, related to March 1972. It showed, the secretary said, an increasing error rate on the part of the states. Indeed, in about 25 percent of the cases there was some degree of error. Moreover, in the then most current full sample of available state data (June-December 1971) 21 states failed to review at least 85 percent of the required AFDC sample cases. For March 1972, in the AFDC subsample, the ineligibility national rate was 6.8 percent of total cases and an overpayment rate of 13.8 percent of total cases. In the adult programs—aged, blind, and disabled—the ineligibility rate was 4.9 percent and overpayment rate, 9.7 percent. Underpayments ranged from 7.6 percent of AFDC to 5.6 percent of the adult cases.

The secretary broke down the savings coming from the cutback program: For fiscal 1974 the federal government should save $456 million, and the states, $364 million. It should be noted, however, that the secretary's figures have been subject to challenge.[26]

The effect of the federal cutback on the states probably would be substantial. An attack was mounted seeking basically the same goals, namely, to dissuade HEW from implementing the cutback and, in any event, to strike at those fair hearing rules that seemed to have high costs attached to them. The attack was more than alternative pleading (i.e., if the HEW cutback occurs, then let there be an easing of the fair hearing rules). Rather, the attack was one designed to strike at the rules as such; the cutback merely provided added impetus.

Attack itself proceeded on two independent albeit related fronts: legal action and conference. First, counsel was retained by 34 states. (It may be significant to note that California and New York were not among the 34 listed states.) A brief in the form of comments was submitted to HEW on January 15, 1973.[27] It is not our purpose to review that brief in toto but instead to state what appear to be some of its essential points: The welfare system itself is bad; it is chaotic; the problem is not with recipient "cheaters" nor with bad administrators.[28] HEW has long recognized that a "certain minimum amount of error" will exist. Toward that end, an official 3 percent tolerance level on incorrect eligibility determinations was sanctioned.[29] HEW contributes to the eligibility error rate by requiring use of the "simplified method for the determination of eligibility"[30]—a method, it must be added, that some states such as New York apparently are not following. Decision on initial application (except for disability) is to be made quickly, within 30 days,[31] and, except where obvious inconsistencies occur in the application, the state is denied the right of verification.[32] At that point the brief launched into the fair hearing

25

rules without noting that existing federal regulations, as well as those proposed, did not suggest a withdrawal of federal aid for those ineligible cases under contest. There seemed an implicit argument in the brief, by its organization and statement, that the federal government was overly taxing the states; all was weighted in favor of the recipients. The brief recited the difficult fair hearing rules:

> Once an applicant is placed on the welfare rolls, the federal regulations make it very difficult either to remove him or to reduce the level of his assistance payments. First, a 15-day notice must be provided in every case where the agency proposes to terminate, suspend, or reduce assistance to any recipient. 45 C.F.R. §205.10(a) (5) (i). If a conference with the agency is requested during the 15-day period, it must be granted. 45 C.F.R. §205.10 (a) (5) (iii). In any case, assistance payments must be continued without reduction until the 15 days have run or, if a hearing is requested, until a decision has been rendered. 45 C.F.R. §205.10 (a) (5) (iii) (a) (1); APA-PRG-4 §III-E, F (March 31, 1972). Thus, despite discovery of the error, an incorrect payment level and even assistance to an ineligible recipient must be continued for at least 15 days in every case, and may have to be continued for as long as 75 days, if a hearing is requested.[33]

The effect of these federal regulations, the brief stated, is not only to foster but in many case to require erroneous payments. Some data were offered in support of the high cost claims. In June 1972 New York City's welfare agency, the Human Resources Administration, paid nearly $5 million to recipients whose cases were marked for closing or for reduction of grants but where HEW fair hearing regulations required that the action be delayed. In 1971 the Michigan welfare agency paid about $450,000 to recipients awaiting negative action hearings: "The initial decision of the local agency was reversed in only about 8 percent of a recent sample of Michigan cases. Thus, most of that amount was erroneously paid."[34]

In the second aspect of the attack, what seemed implicit in the argument of 34 states concerning fair hearings surfaced explicitly in "informal" conferences between the Committee on Proposed Quality Control Regulations of the National Council of the American State Public Welfare Administrators (APWA), HEW's Social and Rehabilitation Service (SRS), and the U.S. Office of Management and Budget. First, however, a word of background to those meetings should be given, for it provides some insight into the important "informal" structure of the Social Security Administration.

A little more than a week after then-HEW Secretary Elliot
Richardson promulgated the proposed cutback regulations, HEW Undersecretary John Veneman met with APWA's National Council to an-
nounce an extension of time for filing comment. Undersecretary
Veneman suggested that the added time might be used by the state
administrators to work with HEW in an effort to develop "a constructive alternative" to the proposed regulation. This included the identification of existing federal regulations that contribute to the problem
of improper payments. The National Council responded by appointing
a special committee, the Committee on Proposed Quality Control
Regulations, to work with HEW. That committee met and drafted a
memorandum of observations and recommendations that was submitted to SRS and used as a basis for discussion.

The committee memorandum itself is considered confidential
although its terms were made known. About half of the six-page
memorandum deals exclusively with the fair hearing regulations.
Other portions of the memorandum touch on matters relating in a
real sense to fair hearings. At no point is supporting data offered
for the recommendations made. The proposals are listed seriatim:

Initital eligibility:
    (a) State verification of applicants should be per-
        mitted.
    (b) The 30-day period for final action on eligibility
        should be extended to 45 days.
    (c) States should be allowed to recover past over-
        payment by means of reducing current payments.

Fair Hearings:
    (a) Fair hearings should only be required where they
        are called for specifically by statute.
    (b) Adherence to procedural due process should be
        that only called for by the courts.
    (c) Local rather than state fair hearings should be
        held prior to the reduction, discontinuance, or
        suspension of grants.
    (d) The 15-day advance notice requirement should be
        revised.
    (e) Continued aid should be altered if the applicant
        furnishes information that calls for such action
        and understands the effect of such action.
    (f) Continued aid should be discontinued in cases of
        "admitted fraud."
    (g) Continued aid of a single unattached person should
        be discontinued when that person has been insti-
        tutionalized or accepted by another jurisdiction;

or receives a large lump sum award from Work-
men's Compensation or Social Security.

(h) State agencies should be permitted to hold checks
pending receipt of a request for a fair hearing, or
the federal government should pay 100 percent in
any case in which the agency's action is upheld.

It was not unusual for APWA to have discussions with SRS. Indeed, regular, frequent conferences are held to allow for an exchange
of views. Based upon past informal practice, it seems that Undersecretary Veneman's invitation could not be considered unexpected.

SRS, however, does not meet regularly and frequently only with
APWA. It also meets with the National Welfare Rights Organization
(NWRO) on the same basis. NWRO attempts to be a national organization of welfare recipients, supported partly by membership dues and
partly by foundation grants. Under contract to agencies of the government, it has done behavioral research relating to welfare recipients.
But it is not dependent on the federal government for its budget. For
legal advice, NWRO often calls upon the Center on Social Welfare
Policy and Law, a legal services resource organization supported
by the Office of Economic Opportunity.

Repeatedly, when HEW fair hearing regulations were proposed,
published, and applied, many states objected vociferously. As the
result of a request to Secretary Richardson that the regulations be
reconsidered, HEW program and legal staff met with state representatives in April 1972. In a meeting in May 1972 HEW staff con-
veyed orally the concerns of the states. NWRO's minutes of the
meeting, compiled by the Center on Social Welfare Policy and Law,
reflect the two chief issues as being (1) continued assistance pending
fair hearing decision and (2) the 15-day advance notice hearing requirement. NWRO addressed itself to those issues in the following terms:

(a) Any major change in fair hearing policy should be
preceded by a public hearing. At such hearing the
states should bear the burden of proof in arguing
for a change.

(b) In any event the fair hearing rules should not be
changed until they have been given a chance to
work and to be tested.

(c) "NWRO articulated extreme concern that HEW might
be willing to accept the undocumented complaints of
the State representatives at face value. It was suggested that HEW could not accurately inform the
Secretary of any State problems before allegations
made by the States had been supported by evidence."[35]

When the states made their specific proposals in December 1972 for changes in HEW's fair hearing regulations, SRS orally discussed the proposals with NWRO. The reaction of NWRO was the same as in May. But there was this difference: It appeared rather certain that the fair hearing regulations would be changed, that at least some of the states' objections to those regulations would be met.

In a sense the writing was on the wall for the NWRO to see. On October 30, 1972, H.R.1 came into effect after President Nixon's proposals for family assistance payments (FAP) failed.[36] It is not our purpose to detail the specifics of H.R.1 or FAP. It will suffice to note that, except for AFDC, the family and adult welfare programs previously in state hands were now federalized. Effective January 1, 1974, the federal government would handle on a uniform basis programs for the aged, blind, and disabled.

In at least two respects H.R.1, as an expression of congressional opinion, touches fair hearings. (It must be remembered that state programs covering aid to the aged, blind, and disabled also were covered by the fair hearing regulations.) First, once the federal program is under way, eligibility will no longer be determined by declaration, by the do-it-yourself method presently applicable to state programs. Rather, eligibility will be granted only after verification. Moreover, penalties are imposed on recipients for failure to report changes in circumstance.[37] The statute requires "reasonable notice and opportunity for a hearing" on "determination[s] . . . [of] eligibility . . . or the amount of benefits,"[38] but it is silent on the issue of prior notice and hearings. The statute leaves open the question, apparently in part for administrative determination as to whether aid will be continued pending a hearing. (The Court in Goldberg dealt only with state action, not federal action.) Furthermore, findings of fact at the hearing are deemed conclusive. In all other respects judicial review is allowed.[39] Second, an interim period before federalization is set out in H.R.1. During that time special provision is made as to fair hearings for state-supervised, locally administered jurisdictions. They are specifically permitted to conduct local rather than state evidentiary hearings.[40] The Senate Finance Committee report clearly attempted to modify HEW fair hearing regulations by bringing them closer to the constitutional minima laid down by the Court in Goldberg: "The [Senate Finance] Committee provision is designed to assure that the appeals procedure is handled expeditiously by the States and also to assure that the appeals are not made frivolously."[41]

There can be no doubt that in H.R.1, as applied to the newly federalized categorical aids programs, Congress intended to and did modify HEW fair hearing regulations. Moreover, as to federal operations beginning in 1974, H.R.1 left open an area for the exercise

29

of administrative discretion. The statute, it was pointed out, was silent on whether benefits must be continued before and during the fair hearing itself. The argument could be made, and there would seem to be some strong basis in it, that Goldberg v. Kelly requires continuation of benefits, that there surely ought to be no difference as far as due process is concerned in the fact that the aid program is federalized and not under the control of the states.

Apparently, however, there is considerable feeling within the Social Security Administration that there is a difference in due process requirements depending on whether the program is administered by the federal or state government. Those so arguing note the only Supreme Court decision in point, Richardson v. Wright, decided more than 35 years after the establishment of the Social Security Act.[42] The decision is a one-paragraph per curiam opinion dealing with Social Security's disability program. It has strong dissents offered by four justices.

In Richardson v. Wright the claimant charged a cutoff of benefits before fair hearing. Goldberg v. Kelly was invoked and appeal taken. Shortly before oral argument before the Supreme Court, HEW revised its regulations to require that a recipient of benefits be given notice of a proposed suspension and the reasons therefor, plus an opportunity to submit rebuttal evidence. The Court said:

> In the light of that development, we believe that the appropriate course is to withhold judicial action pending reprocessing, under the new regulations, of the determinations here in dispute. If that process results in a determination that Mr. Wright is entitled to disability benefits, there will be no need to consider his constitutional claim that he is entitled to an opportunity to make an oral presentation. In the context of a comprehensive complex administrative program, the administrative process must have a reasonable opportunity to evolve procedures to meet needs as they arise. Accordingly, we vacate the judgment of the District Court of the District of Columbia, 321 F. Supp. 383 (1971), with direction to that court to remand the case to the Secretary and to retain jurisdiction for such further proceedings, if any, as may be necessary upon completion of the administrative procedure.[43]

In a sense the new regulations of HEW were precisely the same as those of New York, which were struck down in Goldberg v. Kelly.

The Secretary seriously misconstrues the holding in Goldberg. The Court there said that "the pretermination hearing has one function only: to preduce an initial determination of the validity of the welfare department's grounds for discontinuance of payments in order to protect a recipient against an erroneous termination of his benefits." 397 U.S., at 267. The Secretary does not deny that due process safeguards fulfill the same function in disability cases. In Goldberg, the Court held that welfare recipients were entitled to hearings because decisions to discontinue benefits were challenged "as resting on incorrect or misleading factual premises or on misapplication of rules of policies to the facts of particular cases." Id., at 268. The Court expressly put aside consideration of situations "where there are no factual issues in dispute or where the application of the rule of law is not intertwined with factual issues." Id., at 268 n. 15. However reliable the evidence upon which a disability determination is normally based, and however rarely it involves questions of credibility and veracity, it is plain that, as with welfare and old age determinations, the determination that an individual is or is not "disabled" will frequently depend upon the resolution of factual issues and the application of legal rules to the facts found. It is precisely for that reason that a hearing must be held.

It remains quite another matter, however, to argue that the Supreme Court, as such, specifically upheld the constitutional validity of HEW's disability regulations. Prima facie, all the Court said was that it would not consider the constitutional question of due process. Nevertheless, within the Social Security Administration there seems to be some strong feeling that the Supreme Court has endorsed an administrative practice of more than 35 years.

The argument of the states for relaxing HEW fair hearing regulations now has received a rationale to support money bargaining with the federal government: Congress as a matter of public policy has declared in H.R.1 that HEW's fair hearing regulations should extend no further than what is required by the Supreme Court. The Court has not strictly adhered to Goldberg v. Kelly. This seemed to be the message of Richardson v. Wright, at least in the minds of three justices. Why should the federal government require more of the states than it requires of itself? A fortiori, why should the states do more in the context of a federal budget squeeze? Finally, in the context of a President committed to return power to the states, how can the discriminatory federal policy be justified?

There are two general observations coming from the discussion of the federal budget, AFDC, and fair hearings:

1. There is a fairly deep infrastructure within HEW for consulting with the relevant interest groups before any major policy change is initiated. The federal budget was the catalyst that led to serious HEW review of fair hearing practices, and it appears that Congress, with the enactment of H.R.1, and the HEW-perceived Supreme Court deviation from Goldberg have provided the rationale for change.

2. More generally, perhaps, but no less important is the need to recognize that administrative regulations do not always have the same permanence as Supreme Court decisions. Nor are administrative regulations adopted or modified for the same reasons that lead a court to a given decision. It is true that the HEW fair hearing regulations codified and went beyond the due process criteria of Goldberg. It is also true that the federal government and the states, both caught in a budget squeeze, have worked rather hard for an accommodation that has reflected itself in modified fair hearing regulations.

NOTES

1. 42 U.S.C. §§2(a)(4), 402(a)(4), 1002(a)(4), 1402(a)(4), 1602(a)(4).

2. That change really came before Goldberg v. Kelly. See 397 U.S. 257, Ch. 1, note 3.

3. 397 U.S. 254 (1970).

4. Id., at 264-65.

5. Id., at 269.

6. Id., at 270-71.

7. Id., at 271.

8. 45 C.F.R. §205.10.

9. Id., at 258: "Even assuming that the constitutional question might be avoided in the context of AFDC by construction of the Social Security Act or of the present federal regulations thereunder, or by waiting for the new regulations to become effective, the question must be faced and decided in the context of New York's Home Relief program, to which the procedures also apply."

10. 45 C.F.R. §205.10.

11. 45 C.F.R. §205.10(a).

12. 45 C.F.R. §205.10(a)(5)(iii).

13. See text, note 7 supra.

14. 45 C.F.R. §205.10(a)(5).

15. 45 C.F.R. §205.10(a)(3).

16. Both states have sued HEW. The Arizona case is presently before the U.S. Court of Appeals for the Ninth Circuit. On petition from Arizona the federal district court for the District of Arizona entered a temporary and later permanent injunction prohibiting HEW enforcement of the fair hearing rules. See Richardson v. State of Arizona (9th Cir. No. 72-2610). Arizona particularly objected to the grant of hearing on issues dealing with changed state law or policy. North Carolina's attack on the regulations is far more comprehensive.

17. Almenares v. Wyman, 453 F. 2d 1075, 1087-88 (2d Cir. 1971).

18. Richardson v. Wright, 40 U.S.L.W. 4332 (Feb. 24, 1972).

19. 397 U.S. 280, 282 (1970).

20. Id., at 283.

21. Id., at 284.

22. Appendix to the Budget for Fiscal Year 1974 at 441-42.

23. Hearings on Social Security and Welfare Proposals before House Committee on Ways and Means, 91st Cong., 1st Sess., pt. 1, at 120 (1969).

24. 37 Fed. Reg. 25853.

25. 37 Fed. Reg. 27636-7 (Dec. 19, 1972).

26. Letter from Henry A. Freedman, Director, Center on Social Welfare Policy and Law, to Professor Baum, Apr. 26, 1973.

27. "Comments on the Proposal to Reduce Federal Support for Public Assistance Programs on Behalf of the Following States and their Public Welfare Departments: Alaska, Arizona, Arkansas, Colorado, Florida, Georgia, Hawaii, Idaho, Illinois, Iowa, Kansas, Louisiana, Maryland, Massachusetts, Michigan, Minnesota, Mississippi, Montana, Nebraska, Nevada, New Hampshire, New Mexico, North Carolina, Ohio, Oklahoma, Pennsylvania, Rhode Island, South Carolina, South Dakota, Texas, Utah, Vermont, Virginia, and the Territory of the Virgin Islands" (Jan. 15, 1973).

28. Id., at 14.

29. 45 C.F.R. §205.20(c)(5). Three percent relates to number of cases. A 5 percent tolerance level is allowed both for over and underpayments.

30. Id.

31. 45 C.F.R. §206.10(a)(3); see Rodriguez v. Swank, 318 F. Supp. 289 (N.D. Ill. 1970), aff'd, 403 U.S. 901 (1971). The comments of the 34 states note that the 30-day requirement "when rigidly enforced, inevitably requires that some eligibility determinations be made before all the necessary data are in hand. In one state, for example, 26 percent of all eligibility determinations are made within the last eight of the allotted 30 days, many on the thirtieth." Note 55, supra, at 27-28.

32. 45 C.F.R. 205.20(a)(3).

33. Note 55, supra, at 28.

34. Id., at 29.

35. 3 Welfare Law, Center on Social Welfare Policy and Law, "Report on Meeting with NWRO Representative on Fair Hearings," at IX-83 (1972).

36. P.L. 92-603, 92d Cong. (October 30, 1972).

37. Section 1631(b), (e)(1)(A)(B).

38. Section 1631(c).

39. Section 1631(c)(3).

40. Section 407(a).

41. Report of the Senate Finance Committee, "Social Security Amendments of 1972," S. Rep. No. 92-1230, 92d Cong., 2d Sess. 451 (Sept. 26, 1972). These comments are included only to express the mood of Congress.

42. Richardson v. Wright, 40 U.S.L.W. 4232 (Feb. 24, 1972).

43. Id.

The previous chapters established a perspective for viewing the AFDC fair hearing. This chapter is concerned with the hearing itself. First, we shall describe the process of decision making with some emphasis on the decision maker of initial contact. Next, the focus will turn to a profile of the AFDC recipient. Using statistical data, we will attempt to answer the question of whether the AFDC recipient profile is in harmony with the stereotype that some may have. Moreover, understanding the nature of the recipient should provide better comprehension of the demands likely to be made on the fair hearing process. For example, if the recipient is long-term, apt to be on the rolls for lengthy periods, there may be a greater willingness to contest adverse decisions.

Closely related to the statistical data concerning the AFDC recipient are the data covering the fair hearing process itself. Cries of alarm have come from many states: the HEW rules are said to be imposing a heavy burden on an already strained system. The National Center for Social Statistics (SRS-HEW) now has collected some data on the fair hearings. How many are exercising their right to a fair hearing? Are they represented? If so, are they represented by counsel or friend? If representation is by counsel, has the responsibility largely been assumed by OEO legal services units? In view of what appears to be presidential opposition to OEO, what is the future for such representation?

There then is the question as to how the fair hearing system is used and, perhaps, abused. In a system that to some extent is uniform but in other ways manifests practices peculiar to 50 different jurisdictions, we can only offer some general observations of the system's use and some examples of its abuse.

Finally, there is the matter of state evaluation of fair hearings. It is true that many states have reacted specifically and sharply to the HEW fair hearing rules. However, the point was made earlier that the APWA submission to HEW for rule modification offered no underlying factual data to support the recommendations. Does that mean no useful evaluations have been made? The answer is a rather clear "no." New York City has an Office of Evaluation in its Human Resources Administration. Work has been done on fair hearings. We shall describe that work.

DECIDING INITIAL QUESTIONS OF BENEFITS

It is not a highly trained social worker, sensitive to the needs and capacities of individual families, who decides initial questions of benefits. The Social Security Act, the HEW regulations,[1] and the guidelines have assigned that task to eligibility technicians. Operating under a system of declaration rather than verification, HEW, it is recalled, has placed emphasis on the simplified reporting form. No social worker is needed to handle this form. The HEW guides state:

> An essential component of the simplified method is the differential use of an appropriately trained staff. Staffing considerations involve the use of sub-professionals, the development of career ladders, and the establishment of specialized units. Functional task analysis assists in grouping tasks in terms of their content and the education and experience levels required by that content.
>   The simplified method offers potential for use of a variety of skills. The skills of an effective eligibility worker, for example, while no less important, are quite different from those of the worker who gives social services. Carefully planned staff training takes cognizance of this difference in function. It is appropriate that training schedules developed by the State relate to the function of the worker group involved in training. Trained staff are then used differentially.[2]

Initial recipient contact is with the eligibility technician assigned to a line function categorized in welfare departments as income maintenance. It is the eligibility technician, frequently a person with no greater formal education than a high school degree, who is the first point of contact in determining whether a claimant is placed on the rolls and whether existing benefits should be modified or terminated.
    Consider the enormity in sheer volume of the eligibility technicians' task in a city such as New York. There are approximately 1.5 million persons dependent on categorical aids in the state of

New York. Most of these fall within AFDC, and most of the recipients, a total of 1.2 million, are resident in New York City. On a monthly average in the city, about 20,000 AFDC cases are terminated and another 20,000 are reduced.[3] To handle this flow, the city Human Resources Administration employs an income maintenance staff of 2,500 and another 500 supervisors. And, said the unit head of that staff, "there are always between 150 to 200 vacancies which we are now trying to fill as fast as we can."[4]

In New York City the eligibility technicians are given an orientation and training course of two or three weeks to familiarize them with their job function. It seems that line officers, those under whom the eligibility technicians work, have no firm understanding of precisely what goes into that training program; that is subject to the jurisdiction of another department.[5] Once on the job, the technician is not subject to ongoing, intensive, central review. That was tried by New York City. While the quality of disposition improved, the heavy price of backlog was paid. As a result, decentralization was ordered.[6] In 1972 primary responsibility for case disposition fell to 44 centers supervised by office managers and assistant managers[7] who sometimes would make spot checks to ensure, for example, that claimants did receive appropriate advance notification of an intent to suspend, reduce, or terminate benefits.[8]

However, no change in benefits would occur on instructions of the income maintenance specialist alone; that specialist's supervisor would have to concur.[9] Then written authorization would be forwarded to the central unit issuing benefit checks. Authorization for benefit reduction or termination, at least before Almenares v. Wyman,[10] could and frequently did come without advance notice of right to a fair hearing.

Yet even today, without in any way imputing bad intent on the part of the city Human Resources Administration, there is no small question as to whether that agency can comply with the Court's order and the HEW regulations concerning advance notice. In a deposition taken from the city Director of Income Maintenance Programs, Planning and Services, a few months after the Court's interim injunction in Almenares v. Wyman requiring compliance with the then less rigid state's advance notice requirements before termination or reduction of benefits, it was indicated that 12,000 notices of intent to reduce or terminate benefits are sent monthly. This figure must be contrasted with the monthly terminations numbering 20,000 plus the monthly reductions numbering 20,000.[11] It is true that notice need not be sent under certain very limited conditions. It is at least questionable whether those conditions justifying not sending notices existed in all or most of the 28,000 monthly cases (i.e., the difference between 12,000 and 40,000).

37

At the problem's root are the difficulties raised by a high volume of cases and quality and quantity of staff. Centralization with a pyramid structure for review will backlog work. Decentralization, even with a mobile review staff, makes it hard for orders and policies to be passed down, received, understood, and acted upon. Moreover, there is the added difficulty of institutional motivation. To some extent the incentives operating upon a welfare agency are not geared to maximizing recipient benefits. Often they are geared, even as official policy, toward effecting welfare savings, sometimes articulated as "taking the cheaters off of the rolls." In such a setting one can safely say that there may be absolute disincentives operating on eligibility technicians, income maintenance specialists, and their supervisors to give an overly high priority to providing recipient advance notice of benefit reduction or termination.[12]

New York City,[13] Los Angeles County,[14] and Alameda County (Oakland),[15] three urban areas with among the highest national caseload volumes and dollar payouts, have not focused their concern on fair hearings as such. Rather, they have addressed themselves to office efficiency; that is, to getting the job done at the lowest possible price. For some agencies this has meant office reorganization. For others it has meant more than reorganization. It has meant redefinition of the income maintenance specialist and either an implicit or explicit rejection of HEW's classification of "subprofessional." (All three urban jurisdictions have conducted intensive agency management studies, and all have undergone major reorganization in the past five years.)

Alameda County, along with other counties in California, had to face the reality of a massive demand for fair hearings, a situation that will be more fully described later. The county attacked the problem in part by establishing the position of Appeals Officer, whose functions include:

1. Reviewing action taken by the eligibility technician carrying the case
2. Returning the matter to the technician if errors are found
3. Discussing the issue(s) with the claimant and explaining the county's position
4. Preparing and presenting the county's position at the fair hearing
5. Preparing instructions to the eligibility technician designed to achieve compliance with the fair hearing award

The agency sought individuals holding degrees in business administration for the position of appeals officer. No longer could the agency put a relatively uneducated technician against a relatively sophisticated legal services attorney. According to the division chief, "Added to the necessary qualifications of the Appeals worker is the ability to present verbal argument and to act in an adversary capacity on behalf of the county's position on an equal footing with attorneys employed by the local Legal Aid Society."[16]

Congress too, recognized the need for flexibility in state organization for decision making. In H.R.1 Congress specifically allowed any state, as to programs for the aged, blind, and disabled, to use "whatever internal organizational arrangement it finds appropriate for this purpose,"[17] thus allowing the mingling of income maintenance with social services.

THE STATE FAIR HEARING

Reflect for a moment on certain statistics: New York City either terminates or reduces the benefits of 40,000 welfare applicants each month, and it receives a total of about 2,000 requests for fair hearings each month. None could dispute the large number of fair hearing requests. By the same token, none could dispute the low percentage of fair hearings relative either to the total number of benefit decreases (5 percent) or to notices of intent to decrease (less than 20 percent). On the whole, the high number of hearings simply is a result flowing from the substantial number of people on welfare.

For New York, as for every other state, the hearings are state, not local, proceedings. Moreover, the decision must be that of the state agency. Having said this, however, there are differences between the states in the conduct of hearings. For our purposes we will provide a brief contrast between New York and Maryland and, more specifically, between New York City and Baltimore, where there are about 100,000 welfare recipients but only 20 to 60 fair hearings are conducted monthly. Finally, we will present California's rather unique effort to expedite the fair hearing process.

In New York City, fair hearings are held at the massive World Trade Center. They are conducted by a relatively highly paid group of lawyers ($17,000 a year) who docket the cases and notify the city and the claimant. The hearings are scheduled at half-hour intervals, but rarely does the examiner meet the schedule. Usually all hearings docketed for 2 p.m. are carried over to the next day. The result tends to bring a kind of police court environment; a sense of hurry pervades the hearings. Claimants certainly are not made to feel that an informal process has been designed to provide for a full, relaxed opportunity to present their case. Nor is the city pleased. It is pressured to prepare its case on short notice. Then it is faced with delay and lost manpower because of the wait to be heard.[18]

At the hearing itself the examiner takes notes. These, together with a proposed decision, are sent to a fair hearing unit within the

39

state welfare department. There the decision is reviewed and often rewritten to comport with one of numerous forms developed by the state.

The decision itself is to be rendered within 60 days following request for a fair hearing. Based upon the sheer volume of litigation, it is not surprising that decision time lags somewhat behind that 60-day deadline. In the interim, of course, the city must continue to pay benefits.

Maryland's procedures contain several points of similarity and some points of difference. There the state is faced with only 20 to 60 fair hearings each month. Two hearing examiners have been specifically designated to handle fair hearings. Both are relatively well paid for state officials (about $15,000 annually). They are housed in the state welfare agency in Baltimore. Hearings are conducted in the offices of that agency.

In Maryland, as a matter of law[19] and implementing regulation,[20] the hearing examiner has the final power of decision for the state welfare agency. The examiner is encouraged to be independent, to question and not merely rely on agency policy manuals that may have no support either in regulation or in statute.[21] Their willingness to exercise such a role is another matter.

Even handling 20 to 60 cases a month between two examiners does not necessarily mean a great deal of leisure time. Cases are postponed; parties are late; a backlog does tend to develop. Yet in the conduct of hearings considerable effort is made to encourage the recipient to speak, to present his case fully—even if that means some intervention by the examiner to help in developing the facts.

It is interesting to note that all cases are transcribed. This is done from a tape recording of the hearing made by the examiner; court stenographers are not used. The transcriptions are not always short. Not infrequently, a hearing involving what may be a simple factual question (i.e., did the claimant pay $X for utilities in a given month—a necessary fact for computation of, for example, food stamp costs) may proceed for nearly two hours. Consider one observed hearing:

First, there was a 40-minute wait for the parties. The paralegal representative for the claimant was 15 minutes late and the claimant 20 minutes late. The city representative, a nonlawyer, forgot that the case had been docketed. A call from the examiner brought him to the hearing, conducted in a bare, windowless room.

It took about 15 minutes for the examiner to go through the necessary introductions and, in this regard, carefully spell out the rights of the recipient in a manner designed actively to involve the claimant in the hearing. The issue related entirely to computation of utility expenses. The paralegal conceded points adverse to his client that the city was not pressing. On the issue itself, the claimant's representative was not prepared. It took questioning from the examiner, after the city had presented its case, to elicit the utility receipts from the claimant. The city's representative said, "If I had seen these receipts there never would have been a problem." The claimant replied that she had shown them to her caseworker. But the caseworker was not the eligibility technician, the income maintenance worker.

The case itself had been delayed at the request of the city on at least two occasions. Indeed, although the city was prepared to go forward with the matter, its representative noted that much of the claimant's underlying file had been "misplaced." The file involved had been misplaced for more than two months. In discussion with the examiner and the city's representative following the hearing, it was noted that "misplaced" or lost files are not unusual. About 17 to 20 percent of welfare files are "misplaced," unavailable, at any particular time.

In many respects the examiner's decision in the Maryland case will be superfluous. The city became aware of new evidence, or so it claimed, at the hearing; it will make the necessary adjustments. At the close of the hearing the city representative, the paralegal, and the claimant were working on a piece of paper to determine just how much food stamps would cost in the future. In dollar figures, $20 a month was involved.

Among the states, California has experienced the largest number of fair hearing requests. The flow rate of California fair hearing requests is uneven, as the following compilation illustrates:

August 1971	2,100
October 1971	9,800
February 1972	2,900
May 1972	8,200
August 1972	5,100
December 1972	3,200
March 1973	5,000

Every request for fair hearing must be prepared as if it will in fact go to hearing; there is no other practical course for the state. Until the issue is finally resolved, once the request is initiated, monies must be paid. In the context of a heavy but uneven flow, it is indeed difficult for California to resolve issues within a short time frame. Robert Best, former chief referee of California, in a letter to the author, wrote:

In California, we hold hearings in approximately seventy locations throughout the state. To have a final decision

41

implemented (i.e., check in hand of the claimant) within
sixty days of filing requires that each request be pro-
cessed not only on a flow basis, but on what, as a matter
of fact, amounts to an expedite basis. Each request
requires immediate attention and there is little opportunity to carry over filings from one month to the next if
the sixty day requirement is to be met. Since no administrative organization can staff to handle on an expedite
basis 8,000 to 9,000 hearings which may occur and have
that staff inactive during those months when hearing
requests are arriving in the area of 3,000 to 4,000 a
month, the end result is that some hearings are carried
over and take longer than sixty days to complete. The
aid pending, therefore, continues well past seventy five
days in some cases.

In California's view, each day that an improper welfare payment
is made means an improper use of tax funds. The challenge, as seen
by the state, is to provide maximum efficiency in dispute resolution
within the context of due process. It is in such a setting that California has initiated new approaches to fair hearings. As described
by Best, they include:

1. Notice. A uniform notice of proposed action was prescribed
   by the state for each county. On the face of that notice is
   a statement of the right to a fair hearing. On the reverse
   side of the notice is an application for a fair hearing that
   includes information as to organizations in the recipient's
   area that may provide assistance in the fair hearing process.
   Notices are mailed in duplicate; the additional copy is the
   request for fair hearing. [It should be noted, however, that
   the notices are in English. There are in California, as in
   New York, very large minority groups in poverty areas,
   and the only language of some of these groups is Spanish.]
2. Calendar. Each request for a fair hearing is placed on a
   calendar immediately upon receipt. Within a few days,
   notices of the time, date, and place of the hearing are sent
   to the claimant and the county. A minimum of 10 days'
   notice is provided prior to hearing.
3. "Q Calender." In counties with large caseloads—such as
   Los Angeles, which accounts for about half of the state fair
   hearing requests—hearing officers are sent in teams varying
   in number from three to eight. Although each claimant is
   assigned a specific hearing time, the hearing officers work
   from a master calendar taking cases on a first-come, first-
   serve basis.

The number of individuals assigned to arrive at each period and the interval between hearings on the calendar is set by a computer program that varies the assignments on the calendar depending upon input such as number of hearings, number of hearing officers, predicted washout rate, and predicted average time of hearing. The computer program itself can generate a variety of calendars, depending on two primary variables: (a) waiting time for claimants and (b) waiting time of hearing officers. On the whole, Best states, programs are designed so that no claimant need wait more than 45 minutes for hearing.

The Q Calender, based on queuing theory, has great flexibility. It apparently has the capacity to operate efficiently whether claimants arrive early or late or even on the wrong day for hearing. Moreover, the hearing officer under the program can take as little or as much time as necessary to complete an individual hearing although, on an average, hearing officers handle about eight hearings per day.

4. Rural counties. Smaller caseloads and greater travel distances do not allow for the operation of the Q Calender. The state has substituted (a) informal cooperation and (b) part-time hearing officers as mechanisms to assist in efficient case disposition. Informal cooperation moves toward substituting recent fair hearing claimants for those who withdraw. The part-time hearing officers are drawn from the rural areas where the hearings are scheduled.

5. Review of decisions. California maintains a staff of hearing officers numbering about 100. To bring uniformity to decision making, the state has established a central review unit to pass upon all proposed decisions within a few days as to accuracy, consistency, and completeness. In addition, to assist in obtaining both uniformity and greater efficiency, "decision aids" were prepared and provided for each hearing officer. These aids include work sheets that allow a hearing officer to prepare a proposed decision on what have been called "routine and repetitive" issues by utilizing standard paragraphs and standard phraseology stored on magnetic tape typewriters.

The effect of California's program in quantitative terms is indeed substantial. In June 1972 there was a total of 34,000 unprocessed fair hearings. Since that time the number of unprocessed fair hearings has been substantially reduced. To illustrate, Los Angeles County, which had the most severe fair hearing backlog problem in 1972, was completely current in 1973. Both the claimants and the state are the beneficiaries of what comes from efficiency. There

is speed, simplified processing, and an opportunity to prepare fully
for the hearing itself. But whether the quality of the hearing or decision is improved by the California process may be an entirely different matter.

RURAL FAIR HEARINGS

The development of this study has centered on the cities. It is
there that the fair hearing process is most often called upon. With
very few exceptions, such as Southern California, rural legal services
have not made much penetration. Still, it is appropriate to discuss
briefly some of the behavioral characteristics of rural populations
as they bear upon fair hearings. In doing this, primary reliance has
been placed on a 1968 field study, before Goldberg v. Kelly and therefore perhaps not entirely in point, conducted by the Duke Law Journal
under the sponsorship of the American Bar Foundation. That study
took for examination a single eastern North Carolina county "typical
of the rural poverty belt."[22]

The following general description can be given of the sample
county: It has a population of 11,000 of whom about half are engaged
in farm-related work and 16 percent in white-collar community service occupations. Of the population, 52 percent is white and 48 percent
black. There are 1,400 families with a median income of $2,300
annually, and 60 percent of the population is below the poverty level
of $3,000 annual income.[23] The county's economic well-being is
dependent largely on tobacco, a highly fluctuating commodity. The
county itself covers 460 square miles. The largest concentrations
of population are in three small communities (populations of 400,
450, and 900) about 10 miles apart from each other on the main county
highway.

Whatever state and federal services there are in the county
operate largely from the county seat. These include the county welfare
department, OEO, the U.S. Agriculture Department, and the county
health department. The county bar has three actively practicing
lawyers, all located in the county seat. (None of the three is black.)
OEO operations in the county do not include legal services, but through
a local economic development corporation OEO does supply "community workers" in mobile units. Of these workers the Duke Law Journal
said:

> The community worker program consists of three Negro
> and two white employees, all natives of the county, who
> visit low income homes in the community in an effort to
> assist families to identify their needs and problems and

44

to take advantage of available assistance programs. The workers stressed that it was not their function to get services for people, but rather to provide motivation and information. The community workers did not, however, evidence the knowledge of service programs observed among the state agency personnel. While they were generally aware of the services available from the health and welfare departments, they had little information on the specifics of the programs and evidenced very little information about aid available through the extension service and the FHA. Only one, for instance, was aware of FHA home loans. Both the workers and the OEO director expressed all of the common misconceptions about the welfare lien generally prevalent among the sample group. One worker in fact reported advising a client that to accept AFDC could result in a lien attaching to her property. The OEO director also reported knowledge of the welfare terminations during the tobacco season but expressed the view that if work was available, nothing could be done. All but one of the workers agreed with this view. The dissenter, who organized the AFDC mothers' demonstration against the welfare department, expressed a desire to appeal the procedure to the state board and complained that the local welfare office would only go through the motions of aiding with the appeal while actually providing no assistance. When asked about the possibility of legal help, however, she stated that under no circumstances would she seek the aid of an attorney with this matter, nor would she ever refer anyone to an attorney for any reason. This OEO community advisor stated unequivocally that legal assistance could never be of value to any poor person. While the other workers did not agree with this view, they also reported that they would not refer a person in the low income group to an attorney because of his inability to pay the fee. None of the workers believed that legal services would ever be provided without charge, no matter how desperate the case, and also evidenced no knowledge of the possibilities of a contingent fee, time payment arrangement, or even the availability of appointed counsel in indigent criminal cases.[24]

The county welfare department was in the control of commissioners who held other full-time jobs. Several of them owned large farms in the area. When summer came, AFDC recipients, including children, were struck from the AFDC rolls. The rationale given by the welfare department was that jobs were available in the county; the AFDC recipients could cut tobacco.[25] More specifically, the summer cutoff worked in the following way: The welfare department asked landlords or farm operators to inform the department of what families would be working for them. The wages that all the members of the family could earn were then computed by the department and the family's benefits were reduced or terminated if the maximum level of income was exceeded. All of the interviewed AFDC recipients reporting benefit cuts during the tobacco season did nothing about it. They merely accepted the welfare department's explanation that benefits must be reduced when work was available.[26]

Beginning with the summer of 1968 the attitude of the community leadership evidenced a change. Several commissioners favored the continuance of AFDC benefits while children were employed; people willing to work, they said, should not be "penalized" and discouraged by a loss of benefits. The county welfare director expressed "similar feelings, adding that she believed the minimum income permitted was too low. During the summer of 1968, income of children under 14 was excluded for the first time in determining the family income. The wages of children over 14 could also be excluded if the family would agree to place the child's wages in a bank account under welfare supervision to be used for educational expenses."[27]

Tobacco growers were able to use AFDC for both incentives and disincentives in the filling out of a labor force. Growers would select employees and then notify the welfare department. The employee and his family would be encouraged to pick tobacco or have their benefits cut. Indeed, the employee and his family would have no practical choice but to pick tobacco so long as they remained in the county; their benefits would be reduced in any event, for they were all employable. On the reward side of the incentive equation, the family was "permitted" to disregard certain portions of the children's income; they, after all, should not be "penalized" for working.

Recipients, if they questioned, did not formally challenge the welfare department's actions. The Duke study made it abundantly clear that most of the recipients had very little idea that they were receiving anything other than "welfare." OEO mobile units provided only general information, and the county welfare department did not provide a great deal more. It may sound strange, but it would not have been beyond belief that the department did not even possess the state regulations. In Maryland, for example, state officials told of counties that had only recently purchased or been supplied with such regulations by the state. And, of course, a volume of regulations on a shelf does not mean there is understanding or a willingness to implement them.

Only two of thirteen interviewees who were denied welfare took any action. When the other eleven were asked why they did nothing about the welfare denial, the common response was: "If the welfare department refuses assistance, there is no use doing anything about it or bothering to see them again." As for the two who took action, consider their approach. One asked his landlord for advice. The landlord advised him "to forget about it," and so the welfare recipient let it go. The other, with the aid of her daughter, spoke with the welfare director, who reversed agency position.[28] In all of this the formal structure of the fair hearing, of notice, of conference, and of a decision on the record do seem rather remote.

PROFILE OF THE AFDC RECIPIENT

The National Center for Social Statistics (NCSS) of HEW's Social and Rehabilitation Service on an ongoing basis collects and publishes data that provide a national profile of the AFDC recipient. Among the more recent NCSS reports is a 1971 two-part study setting forth the demographic, program, and financial characteristics of those receiving AFDC.[29] That study, taking data flowing from assistance payments in January 1971, is important for the stereotype it destroys and the profile that emerges.

The publicly held profile of the AFDC recipient can be described in these terms: The head of household is black and female. The father either is unemployed or has deserted the home. The family itself is large, numbering about five or six. The children probably are illegitimate. The family has been dependent on AFDC for several years and lives in the city.

Against such a profile, consider the statistical summary flowing from the NCSS study, which contrasts a month in 1969 with January 1971; Three out of four AFDC families now live in a metropolitan area, an increase from 72.4 percent in 1969 to 74.4 percent in January 1971. There was a decrease in black families receiving AFDC; even in 1969 blacks did not constitute a majority of the total:[30]

Race	1969(%)	1971(%)
White	48.1	48.3
Black	45.2	43.3
American Indian	1.3	1.2
Other	0.6	0.7
Unknown	4.8	6.5

For the average AFDC recipient the time on assistance has become shorter, and there are more first-time recipients. The median time on assistance, from the latest opening of the case until the study month, dropped from 23 to 20 months. A relatively low percentage of the total, 17.7 percent, have received AFDC on a long-term basis (defined as in excess of five years). In January 1971 families receiving AFDC for the first time were 65.8 percent of the total.

The family units were small in number and the heads of household relatively young in age. Families with only one or two child recipients increased from 49.6 percent in 1969 to 54.2 percent in 1971. Mothers under age 25 increased from 24.2 percent in 1969 to 28.2 percent in 1971. The proportion of all children under age 6 rose from 32.5 percent in 1969 to 34.3 percent in 1971. Families with one or more illegitimate children decreased from 45.1 percent in 1969 to 43.5 percent in 1971.

On the economic side, reflecting the young age of the mothers and their children, 37.1 percent did not work because they were needed in the home. The recipients often were not drifters: Of the AFDC recipients, 40.3 percent had never lived outside their present state or residence and 27.5 percent of the mothers had completed high school.

A significant number of the families surveyed appeared to be fully dependent on AFDC for the limited time of its use. They were interested primarily in receiving their allowance checks and had relatively little interest in the multiple related service programs connected with AFDC. The services they were interested in concerned employment opportunities and training.

The question now is to what extent AFDC payments did meet stated need. In this regard it is important to recall the role of the states in the supervision of AFDC: They are to determine individual need and then to allocate funds to meet all or only a portion of that need. Table 3 shows the national needs averages compiled by NCSS.

AFDC families can earn money. Their income from work will not be fully offset against their allowance; they are permitted to deduct, for example, employment costs and child care during the parents' working hours. A total of 34.7 percent of AFDC families had some nonassistance income in 1971, netting an average amount of $94.65 per family.[31] Yet in 1973, at the time of the study, 46 percent of AFDC families had some unmet need (the difference between need and income from all sources). That unmet need averaged $64.60 per family each month.[32] This unmet need existed despite the fact that recipients by regulation are permitted to keep $30 per month and one-third of any earned income. Moreover, all student-earned income may be retained.

TABLE 3

National Needs Averages
(in dollars)

Number of Child Recipients	Average Monthly Requirement of Families with Specified Number of Adult Recipients[a]		
	None	One	Two
Total	132.97	244.48	313.75
One	78.38	167.72	224.61
Two	132.70	216.53	266.51
Three	183.36	261.11	298.17
Four	216.86	303.21	339.40
Five	286.81	333.16	361.91
Six[b]	301.07	372.48	392.56
Seven or more	—	434.17	466.06

[a]In 9.9 percent of AFDC families there was no adult recipient; in 77.2 percent, one adult recipient; in 12.9 percent, two adult recipients.
[b]Six or more child recipients.

Source: Findings of the 1971 AFDC Study, Dep't. HEW Pub. No. SRS-72-03756, NCSS Report AFDC=1(71), Dec. 22, 1971, pt. 1, at 3.

From the statistical summary, bearing in mind some real questions concerning its validity, certain generalizations may be in order, some of which touch upon the fair-hearing process. AFDC applies to a larger number of whites than blacks. Most of the recipients are young with small families, and they are more or less fully dependent on AFDC for an interim, not a lengthy, period of time (average of 20 months). They have a need for their allowance check, but no particular felt need for attendant social services unless they bear upon obtaining a job.

Most of the AFDC recipients will not return to welfare once they come into the mainstream of economic life. Their concern with AFDC is immediate and not long-term. They may be compelled to use the fair hearing process once or even twice, but probably no more often than that. Once their initial eligibility is determined, although they are told to report any variance in income to the eligibility specialists, their files will not be subject to agency-initiated review for six months. During the average recipient's stay of 20 months on the rolls, there will be no more than three agency reviews. And, aside from voluntary recipient submissions and questions derived from the implementation of agency policy, it is really only out of these reviews that challenges to recipients arise, and with them the demand for fair hearings.

Statistically, the greater number of recipients need AFDC only on a short-term basis. By their own efforts they will remove themselves from the roles. Yet this is not to deny that a very large number of persons are dependent on AFDC on a long-term basis. They may have great need to have available a dispute-resolving mechanism, for they may be compelled to use a large number of grant programs (such as food stamps) and social services in support of AFDC. Out of this complex may come many points of conflict. So it may be that some states such as Maryland are seeking not to contract but rather to expand their social services.

THE NUMBER OF FAIR HEARINGS AND RECIPIENT REPRESENTATION

As statistics have been gathered relating to the AFDC recipient, so, too, gross data have been compiled on varying aspects of the fair hearing. The NCSS report for January-June 1970 was the first government effort to publish statistical information on hearings in public assistance since 1954. During that six-month period (with California not reporting) there was a national total of 19,400 requests for fair hearings.[33] This figure more than doubled for the reporting period January-June 1971, when a total of 46,500 requests for fair hearings were received. Three states—California, New York, and Texas—accounted for slightly more than half (53.5 percent) of all hearing requests filed by applicants and recipients.

Fair hearings, it is recalled, presently cover all categorical aid programs and medical assistance. AFDC accounted for the largest number of requests for hearings, 44.1 percent; the adult categories accounted for 47.5 percent; and medical assistance for 8.4 percent). Requests for hearings did not always result in fair hearings taking place. Twelve states, including California and New York, reported that more than one-half of their hearing requests were disposed of without a formal hearing. The nature of that disposition generally, and by a considerable margin, was not in favor of the claimant. Indeed, where the matter was disposed of without hearing, the largest category was that of "request withdrawn," although this did not always mean a decision against the claimant. Where the matter went to hearing, the claimant generally, and by a considerable margin, lost. The hearing decision ratio on a national basis for the reporting period January-June 1971 was about three to one against the claimant. (It must be emphasized, however, that the same ratio necessarily means a substantial number of cases were decided in favor of the claimant.)

There are at least a few possibilities that emerge from the relatively poor claimant-win ratio:

1. The claimant was correct in a substantial number of cases.
2. The claimant evidently understood that his claim lacked validity and withdrew the request for hearing.
3. For those matters that went to hearing, the agency was well prepared and able to support its position in fact.
4. For those cases that went to hearing, the claimant was not well prepared.

No doubt there are other possibilities, for the statistics as such are not statements of evaluation. There is, however, one set of statistics that should be read against the number and disposition of hearing requests. That set of statistics relates to representation of claimants at fair hearings. In the data recount supplied by NCSS, the only major state not reporting on representation was New York, which accounted for 5,900 of the total national figure of 7,300 cases not reported as to representation. California and Texas, however, did report. Of 5,700 hearing requests disposed of in California during the reported period, the claimant was self-represented in 3,100 instances. In Texas self-representation was even greater; of 4,500 matters disposed of, the claimant was self-represented in 4,100 instances. The national gross figures and the state-by-state analysis follow the same pattern.

Private attorneys appeared only in about 2 percent of the total number of requests for fair hearings; law students in an even smaller percentage of cases. The broad category of legal aid procedure accounted for about 10 percent of total representation in fair hearing requests. And a word must be said about the broad category of "legal aid procedure." Very often the use of such procedure does not mean representation by an attorney. Rather, the claimant is apt to be represented by a paralegal trained over a period of several weeks by an OEO-funded agency. There are no formal educational requirements laid down for a person to become a paralegal. In terms of background, the paralegal may be another AFDC recipient—it is interesting to note that by and large AFDC recipients who serve as paralegals are female—or a youngster of twenty from an upper-middle-income family with a college education.

In such a setting the role of the private bar and OEO-funded legal services certainly must be questioned. (Judicare, the publicly funded program allowing the use of private lawyers is discussed briefly below.) The statistics seem to indicate that no meaningful role is played by the bar; claimants tend to represent themselves. Yet observation indicates that the statistics tell only part of the story. Consider first the number of fair hearing requests. What has brought about a doubling of requests from the January-June 1970 period to the January-June 1971 period? The answer in no small measure springs directly from OEO legal services at the community level. In numerous instances, and sometimes as part of a strategic drive (as we shall see), OEO legal services will encourage and assist claimants in requesting fair hearings.

Beyond informing claimants of rights and encouraging the exercise of those rights, OEO legal services groups have been instrumental in establishing and expanding upon the basic right to a fair hearing itself. They have played major roles in planning and executing litigation that established constitutional bases to a fair hearing through arguments of due process and equal protection.[34] They have sought judicial assistance in the proper state enforcement of HEW fair hearing regulations.[35] Through the NWRO they have argued for the promulgation of the HEW fair hearing rules as they now exist, and have attempted to dissuade any retrenchment by HEW. Finally, OEO legal services has made its appearances before congressional committees considering legislation that might affect fair hearings.

The role of OEO legal services at a community level, and especially at a national level through, for example, the Center on Social Welfare Policy and Law, has been significant—not so much for individual claimant representation but for policy involvement that goes to the very structuring of the fair hearing process.

In a very real sense, where OEO legal service action has been effective it can be analogized to the role of the Washington law firm concerned with protecting and promoting the long-term interests of clients through appropriate representations to Congress and administrative agencies, and, where necessary, selective litigation. The effective role of OEO legal services is far removed from the legal aid clinics for the poor of several years ago. Attention is not focused as such upon plea bargaining and arguing the merits of individual cases. Attention more recently has been centered on the system itself.

It is precisely OEO legal services' view of function to which the Nixon Administration objects. The effect of that objection very likely could destroy the OEO legal services function. The New York Times stated on February 11, 1973:

President Nixon included more than $70 million in his 1973-74 budget to fund [a federal legal services] corporation, but the Administration has not yet recommended any enabling legislation to Congress. While the lawmakers wait, the legal services program is being funded

on a month-to-month basis. . . . From its inception, the
legal services program has been a center of political
controversy. In a number of cases, Federal funds have
been used to underwrite law suits by the poor against state
and local governments. These suits have produced shrill
protests from elected officials. . . . Ted Tetzlaff, acting
director of the Office of Legal Services in O.E.O. [said]
he would have to advise his lawyers in the field to stop
accepting new clients if agreement on the future of the
program cannot be reached within the next week or two.[36]

In the meantime the OEO legal services system was losing its
professional staff as its future remained clouded. Yet even if agreement is reached, even if OEO legal services are funded again by the
federal government by means of a national legal service corporation
or otherwise, there is every reason to believe that severe constraints
will be placed upon their policy-playing role. This was made clear
in a White House memorandum, "Issues Concerning Legal Services,"
written by Marshall Boarman, then head of the OEO Legal Services
Office of Program Review, and dated September 1972.

The 57-page memorandum presents a detailed rationale for the
Nixon Administration's approach. In essence, it argues that publicly
funded legal services should be primarily concerned with providing
individual indigent clients with traditional legal aid and that it is,
inter alia, inappropriate for the lawyers in the program to concern
themselves with "test cases" that, if successful, would reform the
system.

The memorandum is divided into five parts: (1) the problem
of accountability; (2) two concepts of legal services; (3) history of
the vacillation in OEO between the two concepts; (4) argument against
the "militant reformist" or "law reform" concept of legal services;
(5) some suggestions for reorienting OEO's legal services program.

Much of the administration's concern is centered around accountability defined in a "broad sense"; it does not merely relate to, although
it does not exclude, the question of who appoints the controlling board
of directors for a legal services corporation. By accountability the
administration means (1) responsiveness in the setting of policy and
(2) the sensitivity of the institution to its various constituencies. It
is in the area of policy making that the administration desires more
thought and action.

It is not the function of this study to probe in depth the arguments
made by the administration for its position, but it is important to
realize that position for its effect on OEO legal services. Moreover,
it is instructive to see the spillover effect on Judicare, both OEO- and
HEW-funded. Judicare, unlike the traditional legal aid office, may be

defined as the delivery of legal services through the use of private attorneys freely chosen by clients.38 Although funded by government (OEO or HEW), there is no operative government control relating to the handling of cases by attorneys freely chosen. Government's role is confined to the eligibility of the client—i.e., poverty level—and to limiting the fee of the attorney to no more than $300 per case and no more than $5,000 per year from the program.

Wisconsin has had the most lengthy experience with Judicare. From 1966, first with the state bar as grantee, and then an independent corporation as grantee, Judicare has operated primarily in 28 mostly rural and sparsely settled counties with a population of 600,000. In 1971 the American Bar Foundation initiated a behavioral study of the program in Wisconsin. In terms of types of problems handled by the private Judicare lawyers, the "family" category stood first, numbering 4,180 cases in the period from June 1966 to May 1971. Among the five categories, listed "administrative" agency matters, (including welfare) ranked last. In that category were 475 matters of which only 37 were identified as welfare cases.39

Yet what of the welfare matters handled by the private lawyers? Did they shy away from controversial issues? After all, these were private lawyers being paid with federal and state funds. The ABA interim report stated:

> The question whether the lawyers had ever turned down controversial or law reform Judicare cases met with a unanimous negative. Several lawyers appeared to be offended by this inquiry and standard responses were, "If it's a case, it's a case—as a lawyer I'm not bothered by such things," or "No, but there simply isn't much like that coming in—mostly routine, private matters." One lawyer stated that he would not handle law reform or appeals under Judicare "because you can't collect much for it," but this appeared to be an abstract response rather than a reference to concrete events.40

The attitude of the private bar was not to reject a test case as such. But there seldom was a need to present such a case, characterized by the interim report as an "impact case." There were at least two reasons for that:

1. To win required no urgent new cause of act-on, no new theory of the case.
2. Members of the private bar did not concern themselves with establishing any given program for the poor that would be fulfilled in part through impact case litigation.

The bar on the whole was content to win individual cases. The win rate came from Judicare clients, who more often than not were plaintiffs. The interim report stated: "The extremely high rate of favorable dispositions of the Judicare cases in our sample is not an aberration but holds for the whole program as well. Some random figures are illustrative: In the first quarter of 1969, 315 cases were resolved—228 won, 79 settled, and 8 lost; in the second quarter, 378 cases were resolved—278 won, 81 settled, and 19 lost."[41]

Judicare has never been a dominant force for the delivery of legal services to the poor. Judicare financed by matching funds from HEW has had even less force. Yet even there, without statement of reason, by omission HEW has declared an intent not to fund Judicare. The rendering of legal services formerly was listed by HEW as among those for which the federal government would provide 75 percent of the dollar cost—should a state adopt an appropriate program. For the forthcoming fiscal year, legal services simply has not been included on the list of services.

These issues and the delay in resolving them were the subject of testimony by Robert W. Meserve, then president of the American Bar Association, before the Subcommittee on Equal Opportunities of the House Committee on Education and Labor, on February 21, 1973, in connection with its consideration of the establishment of a National Legal Services Corporation.

Meserve prefaced his remarks by stating:

The task which this Committee commences with these hearings on legislation to establish a national corporation is both critically important and vitally urgent. I need not dwell on the obvious fact that continued debate without resolution on the important issues before you will seriously damage the program and perhaps critically obstruct the continuation of the legal services movement.
. . .
The pendency of the legislation and the continuing debate over its provisions have resulted in a rudderless course in national program administration. Crucial decisions and policy directives have been postponed because of the continued anticipation that the new structural autonomy of a corporation was just around the corner.

As you will undoubtedly know, the program has been without a permanent director since February 1972, and the National Advisory Committee which has traditionally been the vehicle for advice and oversight by the organized bar was recently disbanded by the Office of Economic Opportunity after not having been convened since

April 1971. The continuation of the program in its current posture must be viewed as a most serious crisis by all concerned. . . .

Restrictions such as those advanced in amendments offered by Senator Murphy in the 90th and 91st Congresses which sought to prevent legal services lawyers from instituting suits against government agencies or officials or allowed governors of the states to control the scope of activities of legal services programs would certainly appear to contravene Canon 5 of the Code of Professional Responsibility which requires that a lawyer exercise independent professional judgment in behalf of a client. The Association vigorously and successfully opposed such provisions in the past and will certainly oppose them in the future.

Several of Meserve's other observations are also pertinent:

As you know, there has been a good deal of controversy surrounding the operations of the Legal Services Program. Unfortunately, the criticism, most of which is unfair and overgeneralized, seems to get more public attention than the excellent client service which the more than 2,300 lawyers currently employed deliver to their previously unrepresented clients on a day-to-day basis. We have all heard the outcry against "law reform" activities of poverty lawyers who, according to the criticisms, neglect the legitimate needs of clients in order to pursue their own agenda of social and institutional reform. A look at the record may help to put that criticism in better perspective.

The Office of Economic Opportunity has released statistics that indicate that the program is currently serving approximately 1,000,000 clients per year. The breakdown of representation indicates further that approximately 42% of the matters involve domestic relations, 18% deal with consumer and job-related problems, 10.5% are housing problems, 9% involve government welfare problems, and 20% are juvenile offenses and other miscellaneous matters. These statistics would seem to accurately reflect the legal problems experienced by the poor and the areas where assistance is most needed. Statistics also indicate that 83% of the matters handled by legal services lawyers are disposed of without litigation. . . .

With regard to the so-called "law reform" activities of legal services programs, it is often overlooked that the mandate from Congress and a review of the program by the General Accounting Office specifically recognize law reform as a legitimate program activity. . . .

In conclusion, the list of accomplishments of the Legal Services Program in the eight years of its operation is most impressive. It has survived adolescence and attained a maturity which argues for a national legal services corporation properly structured so as to assure the continued professionalism of the program which, at the same time, insulates the projects from political pressures. We must have the necessary confidence in the legal profession and the judiciary to assure that the corporation and its grantees will be continually monitored and measured by the professional standards applicable to all the components of our justice system. We must also recognize that legal services to the poor has become an integral component of that total system and must be continued and hopefully expanded and strengthened.

The points made in this section of our study are few but important: Most AFDC claimants do represent themselves in fair hearings. Their win rate is rather low, but this does not mean that the role of the lawyer, and especially OEO legal services, is insignificant. Quite the contrary is true. OEO legal services have played a most important role in shaping the fair hearing process that will best serve the immediate interests of the claimant.

Recall for a moment that most AFDC claimants are on the rolls for only 20 months. It was OEO legal services—in support of the National Welfare Rights Organization—that helped to bring about HEW regulations prohibiting benefit cuts until final state decision, a period of 75 days, two and a half months, probably most of what an individual needs before he would otherwise leave the rolls. It was the same OEO legal services that brought what amounted to compliance proceedings against state agencies to compel enforcement of the HEW regulations. Yet another point should be noted: HEW regulations and OEO policy could have had the effect of keeping some on the rolls who should have been denied payments. A direct result of that, in turn, could have lessened somewhat the amount of income "deserving" claimants would have received. Such is the argument of some administrators. OEO legal services spokesmen replied that the number of ineligibles receiving payment was statistically insignificant in relation to the whole of the welfare class.

OEO legal services influenced the structure of fair hearings in a significant way. It is precisely because of OEO's policy orientation that the president has recommended strict control over the OEO legal services system—if indeed it is to have a future.

Of the private lawyer in fair hearings there is little to say. His role has been most limited. Moreover, whatever role he played through Judicare financed by HEW is scheduled to be eliminated under proposed HEW regulations.[42]

USE AND ABUSE OF THE FAIR HEARING

The AFDC fair hearing process is not a friendly process in which the interests of the federal government, the states, and the individual claimant meld; it is not analogous to the Veterans Administration. Rather, the AFDC fair hearing process, more often than not, is an adversary process; the interests of the state are pitted against those of the individual. Because this is so, pressures are exerted that can cause distortion, leading even to the breakdown of the process itself.

This section is intended only to make the point that the fair hearing process will not always be used fairly. The interests of the parties will push against the process seeking their own ends. The state will strive for efficiency, meaning speedy decisions with low reversal rates. The individual will seek to maximize subsistence benefits. In saying this our intent is not to criticize or evaluate, but only to describe a reality that lawyers fully representing their clients should understand: The processes of justice are not to be obstructed but they are to be used to their appropriate limits in the client's interests. In sum, the lawyer knows that it is the client whom he serves and not, as such, the process.

On the recipient side, fair hearings have been sought by welfare organizations bent on increasing their membership. Such organizations have gone in search of recipients, offering to get them more than they were previously receiving. Then a large number of individual fair hearings have been requested en masse. The welfare agency was placed in real difficulty: The demand for mass individual hearings forced the state agency to adjust radically its existing hearing structure (through, for example, the employment of more examiners) and potentially increased costs. The alternative was to reach a compromise on the individual demands. The Center on Social Welfare Policy and Law described the role of mass individual hearings in New York City:

> Members of welfare rights groups have often filed large
> numbers of fair hearing requests in connection with

campaigns around particular issues, and this device has proved most effective. During the New York City special needs grants campaign in the Fall of 1969, over a thousand fair hearings were requested. Rarely was the hearing completed; rather, the City acknowledged its obligation to make the special grant as the hearing date approached.

Of course, effective use of the fair hearing on behalf of the organization requires substantial preparation by lawyers or lay advocates conducting the hearings to assure that a proper record is made and that recipients have been able to present their grievances as they wish. Because of this demand for trained manpower, it may well be the decision of a group that demonstrations, press conferences, and related public activity are more likely to succeed than the internal pressure which is created by a fair hearing campaign.[43]

California, which faces the largest number of fair hearings, has characterized welfare organization activity directed at the fair hearing process as often abusing the system. Robert Best, former chief referee for California, wrote to the author: "The true . . . problems . . . however, relate to efforts to prolong assistance to ineligible individuals, and to frustrate or jam the welfare administrating system." In his description of the California system, Best elaborated on welfare organization attempts to jam the fair hearing process:

> The first indication of serious problem for California came in the Spring of 1971 when welfare organizations throughout the State, dissatisfied with administrative reforms, announced a "Spring offensive." The stated goals in the literature were 100,000 fair hearing requests and a complete breakdown in the fair hearing machinery. Although the "offensive" fell far short of its goals, hearing requests for the period increased by 50% to 100% each month, and by July, when the offensive had run its course, the backlog of unprocessed hearings in California had increased by over 50% to over 15,000.

For their part, the states sometimes have used the HEW regulations to cut back on the individual right to benefits pending the state fair hearing decisions. The opportunity for "efficiency" apparently exists in the regulatory distinction between fact and policy.[44] If the issue is one of state policy rather than fact, a state may terminate benefits before the state fair hearing decision. By statute, California requires the following: Whenever the state's chief referee determines that a recipient's appeal only raises issues of policy and not issues of fact or judgment, aid is not to be paid pending the state fair hearing.[45]

Citing Goldberg v. Kelly,[46] the constitutionality was challenged of both the HEW regulations allowing the fact-policy distinction and the California statute.[47] Prior to convening the three-judge court, a temporary restraining order (TRO) was issued by the chief district court judge. That order prevented any prehearing terminations or reductions of welfare recipients who had filed timely appeals. At the first hearing before the court, the state moved to modify the TRO. The state argued that the implementation of statute and its attendant regulations in reality would relieve welfare recipients of a pleading burden. Moreover, through regulations the state's chief referee was to receive more factual information relevant to each case, with the result that a more informed judgment between fact and policy might be made.[48] The court accepted the state's argument: In Richardson v. Wright[49] the Supreme Court had "instructed" lower courts to allow agencies to solve their problems if possible.

The state regulations had been in effect since March 16, 1972, pursuant to court order. On September 28, 1972, argument was heard concerning how the regulations had worked. The court found:

> After reviewing all the briefs including regular statistical reports on the effect of the new regulations, the Court concludes that the regulations deny welfare recipients due process according to Goldberg v. Kelly. . . . The Court finds that the regulations work to erroneously deny pre-termination hearings to welfare recipients who have raised factual issues on appeal. For the reasons given below, the Court concludes that new regulations would probably not remedy the errors because of the inherent difficulties in using this fact-policy distinction.[50]

Before going to the court's reasoning, it should be noted the court was "satisfied" that the state regulations would be as effective as possible. The standards seemed to be precise. Yet in its monitoring of fair hearing decisions the court found (1) mistakes in judgment[51] and (2) "what appears to be the State's misuse of these regulations."[52] While the first point (mistakes in judgment) is important, it is the second (misuse of regulations) that is significant for our purposes.

During the period the regulations were in effect, thousands of California welfare recipients had their aid reduced as a result of the new welfare code. Although many of the recipients filed timely notice of appeal from reductions, their benefits were still reduced or terminated prior to any hearing. The court stated, "In the examples presented to this Court, it appears that many of these recipients raised what appear to be factual issues yet still did not receive aid pending a hearing."[53] The state explained the apparent inconsistency: The recipients, even in the cases noted, raised only policy questions: Why? Because, the state argument ran, the chief referee had sufficient factual information in each case to be sure his decision to terminate or reduce benefits was correct. Therefore, it followed, since the decision to terminate or reduce was factually correct, the recipient could only be raising a policy challenge—and the state could terminate or reduce benefits prior to hearing if the issue related to policy. The court held:

> When the Court modified the TRO, it did not foresee that the regulations could be used in this way. This is not to say that the State has purposefully misused the regulations or misled the Court. However, the Court does find that this episode vividly demonstrates the danger of making critical decisions concerning the eligibility of welfare recipients on the basis of the fact-policy distinction. Again quoting from Goldberg v. Kelly, at page 266, where the court was quoting from the lower court decision in that case, " '[t]he stakes are simply too high for the welfare recipient, and the possibility of honest error or irritable misjudgment too great, to allow termination of aid without giving the recipient a chance, if he so desires, to be fully informed of the case against him so that he may contest its basis and produce evidence in rebuttal.' "
>   On the basis of the evidence to date, this Court concludes that the fact-policy distinction is not viable in the welfare context for making the critical determination of whether aid will be paid pending a hearing. The United States Court of Appeals for the Seventh Circuit recently reached a similar conclusion, Mothers' and Children's Rights Organization, et al. v. Sterrett, et al., 467 F. 2d 797 (Cir. 7, 1972), (Slip opinion). Also see Woodson v. Houston, 27 Mich. App. 239, 183 N.W. 2d 465 (1970).[54]

The court emphasized that the state had not purposefully misused the regulations. Rather, what the court seemed to be saying was that the regulations were susceptible to misuse. The state's interest in efficiency was not the same as the recipient's interest in benefits, and the best way to strike a balance between the two interests was to order the full payment of benefits pending the final state fair hearing decision. With this analysis, Circuit Judge Hamlin dissented:

> While it might be that the regulations in question do not guarantee that no mistakes will be made, they are designed to, and reasonably do, provide aid pending fair hearings where factual matters are in dispute. . . . Certainly errors are inherent in any very large scale administrative undertaking and I would expect that the [state] would use every effort to reduce even the small percentage now existing.

Apparently California continues to believe that its fact-policy approach has validity. In a letter to the author dated May 8, 1973, Robert Best, former chief referee for California, stated:

> I must point out that the entire Yee-Litt order was not based on the state's "misuse" of regulations, but rather on what the court found to be a few isolated instances of error. The court specifically indicated that the state had not intentionally misused the regulation. When the state went back into court and challenged the order and the misleading statements upon which it was based, the court refused to review its decision and indicated that the point was not important as the decision rested on the fact that errors were made. It is interesting to note that this order by the Yee-Litt court is based on allegations by the plaintiff that during a time when in excess of 15,000 requests for fair hearings were processed by the state, 49 errors were made in aid pending decisions. Upon review of the 49 alleged errors by the plaintiffs, the state was able to establish only three that were, in fact, errors. While it was true, in most of the instances, that aid pending was denied where factual issues were raised (in several of the 49 cases either no factual issue was raised or aid pending had actually been paid), the court overlooked the fact that the factual issues arose from actions taken many days, and sometimes months, beyond the fifteen day filing period during which aid pending may be authorized.

STATE EVALUATION OF FAIR HEARINGS

From the beginning, Goldberg v. Kelly and more particularly the implementing regulations of HEW have been an object of state concern. Even for those few states that have learned—in the words of some OEO officials—to live with the regulations, there are still points of objection, provisions they would prefer to see modified. In each and every instance the state line of attack is rooted in money costs. This section attempts a brief probe of articulated state objections; that is, in this section we do not question the relationship, the relevance of a money-cost argument to the application of constitutional due process or to the implementing agency regulation that enlarges upon procedural due process.

On September 26, 1972, then HEW Secretary Richardson replied to a letter of "concern" over current federal fair hearing policy from New York City Mayor John V. Lindsay. In his letter Secretary Richardson enclosed what he called a questionnaire addressed to all the states in an effort to aid in an internal HEW review of the fair hearing regulations. That questionnaire is interesting because of its substance, brevity, and title. In its entirety, it read:

Issues Raised by Representatives of the APWA Council of State Administrators

Issue One: A primary cause of the increase in fair hearing requests and the additional costs States are experiencing is due to capricious requests for hearings initiated by persons trying to make unnecessary work and trouble for the agency.

Question: Please provide documentation with regard to any additional costs your State may be incurring due to capricious requests for hearing including, if possible, the numbers of such requests on a monthly or quarterly basis.

Issue Two: Continued assistance pending a fair hearing decision— 45 C.F.R. 205.10(a) (5) (iii) (a) (1).

Question: Please provide documentation with regard to any increased costs involved in continuing assistance in termination, reduction, or suspension cases where a timely request for a fair hearing has been made and an issue of fact or judgment is in dispute.

Issue Three: Fifteen day advance notice requirement—45 C.F.R. 205.10(a) (5) (i) (a).

Question A: In cases of proposed termination, suspension, or reduction, please indicate the number and percentage of conferences that are being held during the 15 day advance notice period.

Question B: Please indicate with supporting reasons in what instances, if any, fifteen days advance notice should not be required.

Issue Four: Fair hearings when the individual is aggrieved by agency policy as it affects his situation—45 C.F.R. 205.10(a) (3).

Question: What is your reaction to the suggestion that States be allowed to establish public proposed rule-making procedures for new policy as an alternative to having fair hearings on questions of policy, thereby limiting hearings to issues of fact or judgment?

Subquestion: Please indicate with supporting reasons whether this public rule-making procedure should solicit written comments only or should also include the opportunity for oral presentations.

Issue Five: Procedure for terminating fair hearing requests when the regulation specifies that the agency shall not deny or dismiss a request for a hearing except where it has been withdrawn by the claimant in writings, or abandoned—45 C.F.R. 205.10(a) (3) (vi).

Question: Please document any dissatisfaction with this area of the regulation, specifying (1) the number and percentage of claimants not showing at a scheduled fair hearing; (2) the reasons given by claimants for such "no shows"; and (3) the number and percentage of claimants who, after missing the first scheduled hearing, request that a second hearing be scheduled.

Issue Six: Requirement that the hearing will be conducted at a time, date, and place convenient to the claimant—45 C.F.R. 205.10(a) (7).

Question: Please indicate with documentation whether claimants are repeatedly postponing fair hearings on the basis that such hearings are not being conveniently scheduled.

Issue Seven: Requirement of group hearings—45 C.F.R. 205.10
                (a) (3) (v).

Question: Do you have any evidence that group hearings are not
                accomplishing their stated purpose to provide for
                consolidation of several hearings on the same issue
                of policy into one hearing because (1) claimants (or
                their representatives) are presenting their own cases
                individually and not as a group, or (2) claimants are
                withdrawing from the group hearing in favor of individ-
                ual hearings?

                Might we again stress the need for specific facts and
                supportive data.

        Mayor Lindsay's letter of concern was based upon a memorandum
and press release of August 14, 1972, from the city's Department of
Social Services (DSS), which particularized and generalized fair hearing issues. The DSS press release called the HEW fair hearing regulations "administrative absurdities" that "strain the public tolerance"
and "stand to defeat any effort to reduce the number of ineligibles on
the assistance rolls." In a New York Times article of the next day,
a Human Resources Administration official was quoted as saying that
the fair hearing regulations do not involve a question of civil liberties
but rather "an uncivil rape of the public treasury."[55]
        The DSS made the following specific charges concerning the
HEW fair hearing regulations:
        1. They required DSS to grant nearly $5 million in assistance
            to cases marked for closing or grant reduction during the
            month of June, as opposed to about $1 million for April,
            the last month before the fair hearing change.
        2. They resulted in grants of an additional $500,000 in June
            to the "mushrooming" number of recipients requesting fair
            hearings.
        3. DSS noted "with alarm" the trend in fair hearing requests
            under the HEW regulations. In April, again, the last full
            month before the regulations came into effect, DSS mailed
            12,500 fair hearing notices. In June, the first full month
            under the regulations, that figure rose to 36,000.
        4. Finally, the DSS release said, "We are now getting persistent
            reports from the welfare community that at least some of
            the clients are already thinking of the procedures as a new
            hustle, which has grave implications for our current program
            to tighten eligibility requirements, especially among our
            addict caseload. This could lead to a widespread cynical

resort to these new procedures and virtually smother the system in paperwork."

The DSS charges, both general and specific, were not based upon a statistical study. Indeed, the Office of Evaluation within the city's Human Resources Administration initiated a statistical study after the charges were made. A preliminary report, covering fair hearing activity for New York from May to October 1972, was completed on December 14, 1972. It answers seriatim, the four charges of DSS. In doing so, the report also gives its methodology.

Now consider the study report's findings:

1. A total of $5 million was not given in assistance to cases marked for closing or grant reduction during the month of June, as opposed to $1 million for April. Rather, the study report stated: "This assertion refers to the new regulation regarding advance notice to clients of proposed action to discontinue, reduce, or suspend a public assistance grant. The data presented . . . indicates that new costs caused by regulatory changes relating to notification totalled approximately $1,331,500 in June and an average of $1,257,188 monthly over the June through September period."56

2. A total of $500,000 was not expended in June for claimants awaiting the state final decision. This charge was related to the HEW regulation requiring continuation of benefits pending the state final decision. The study declared: "Cost of this new aid-continuing provision was about $181,836 in June or about $223,671 monthly over the June to October period."57

3. There is no trend in terms of increased fair hearing requests. The study found that after the June jump to 36,000 there was a tendency to level off. Moreover, the report stated: "the rise in hearing requests corresponds to the increased volume of M3C's [notices of benefit cuts and the right to a fair hearing] mailed to clients, and appeals relating to these notices represent less than 6% of all notices sent. The higher volume of M3C's is due not only to regulatory changes (which account for less than half the increase), but also to the elimination of errors made under the confusing former regulations and to new policy emphasis regarding eligibility and fraud control."58

4. The report rejected the DSS conclusion that frivolous requests for fair hearings were being made. It did so on the basis of the following quantitative findings: (a) The proportion of hearings decided in favor of the claimant has increased under the HEW regulations; (b) aid-continuing cases have remained at a plateau and did not show a trend of continual

increase; (c) the proportion of clients defaulting on scheduled fair hearings has decreased; and (d) the number of conferences conducted by city income maintenance centers (before fair hearings) has doubled.[59]

Based upon a statistical study, the report's final conclusion is that "the rise in hearing requests was due to an increase in legitimate grievances for which public assistance recipients and applicants exercised their right to appeal."[60] In his cover letter to the director of the city Human Resources Administration enclosing the study, the head of the Office of Evaluation wrote:

It is my observation based on information gathered to date that the tone and emphasis of the new [HEW] regulations serve to protect the public against arbitrary and capricious administrative action. I therefore assert that DSS should formally moderate its August 14 position on Fair Hearings and communicate this to HEW and New York community groups concerned with the hearing process.

To date, the position of DSS has not been "moderated." It remains on the whole the same as on August 14. The study conducted after the city's conclusions were announced did find what seemed to be proper use of the fair hearing process at a cost that did not approach the estimates set forth by the city. Yet even the study indicates that there are real costs to the city in the conduct of fair hearings. And, perhaps more important, the fair hearing process limits the city in shaping a flexible welfare policy; it cuts back on the exercise of administrative discretion.

NOTES

1. 45 C.F.R. §205.20(a) (2) (iii) (d).
2. 45 C.F.R. §205.10(a) (3).
3. Deposition of Hilda Hollyer, New York City director of income maintenance programs, planning and service, Almenares v. Wyman, S.D.N.Y. 71 Civ. 3503 at 56 (Feb. 28, 1972); see also New York Times, Mar. 11, 1973, §4, at 1.
4. Id., at 44.
5. Id., at 45-46.
6. Id., at 43-44.
7. Id., at 18.
8. Id., at 22.
9. Id., at 8.

10. 453 F. 2d 1075 (2d Cir. 1971), cert. denied. Substantial restraints were placed on the state and city of New York by the Second Circuit. See 453 F. 2d at 1089.

11. See note 3 supra, at 56.

12. Id., at 76-77.

13. Id., at 14.

14. Interview with David Fullbright, Chief, Appeals Division, Los Angeles County Welfare Department.

15. Interview with Barbara Hellmuth, former Chief, Appeals Division, Welfare Department, Human Resources Agency, Alameda County, California.

16. Letter from Barbara Hellmuth, former Chief, Appeals Division, Welfare Department, Human Resources Agency, Alameda County, California, to Professor Baum, May 14, 1973.

17. P. L. 92-603, 92d Cong. §405 (Oct. 30, 1972).

18. Letter from Jule M. Sugarman, administrator-commissioner, New York City Human Resources Administration, to Abe Lavine, commissioner, New York State Department of Social Services, Nov. 13, 1972.

19. 4a Md. Ann. Code §§253-54 (1971 Replacement Volume). There does exist the right of what can amount to full judicial review — §255.

20. Seven Rules of the Maryland State Department of Employment and Social Services §7.02.09(c) (6)-(9).

21. Interview with Joel Rabin, Assistant Attorney General, Maryland Department of Employment and Social Services.

22. "Project: The Legal Problems of the Rural Poor," 1969 Duke L. J. 495, 497.

23. Id., at 498, 500.

24. Id., at 475-76.

25. Id., at 544.

26. Id. (See also N. Ca. Pub. Assistance Reg. §32 (c) (a): "The net income of all children included in the budget must be counted as a family resource except earnings of children under the age of 14 and those amounts being saved for educational purposes.")

27. Id., at 545.

28. Id., at 547-48.

29. Findings of the 1971 AFDC Study, Dep't. HEW Pub. No. SRS-72-03756, NCSS Report AFDC-1(71), Dec. 22, 1971, pt. 1 at 3. The findings are reported in two parts, "Demographic and Program Characteristics" (here called pt. 1) and "Financial Circumstances (here called pt. 2).

30. Id., pt. 1 at 3.

31. Id., pt. 2 at 5.

32. Id., pt. 2 at 7.

33. Fair Hearings in Public Assistance, Dep't. HEW Pub. No. SRS-72-03257, NCSS Report E-8 (1-6/70), Nov. 10, 1970, at 1. The primary focus of the text draws upon the more current report, Fair Hearings in Public Assistance [January-June 1971], Dep't. HEW Pub. No. (SRS) 72-03253, NCSS Report E-8(6/30/71), May 22, 1971.

34. OEO legal services was involved actively in Goldberg v. Kelly, 397 U.S. 254 (1970).

35. Almenares v. Wyman, 453 F. 2d 1075, (2d Cir. 1971).

36. W. Weaver, "Lawyers Forming Legal Aid Drive," New York Times, Feb. 11, 1973, at 24.

37. M. Boarman , "Issues Concerning Legal Services," Sept. 1972.

38. S. Brakel, Wisconsin Judicare: A Preliminary Appraisal (Chicago: American Bar Foundation, 1972) at 2.

39. Id., at 80.

40. Id., at 87-88.

41. Id., at 96-97.

42. HEW Judicare was established under a demonstration grants scheme. See HEW State Letter No. 1053, Nov. 8, 1968.

43. 3 Welfare Law, Center on Social Welfare Policy and Law, 1972 at IX-189.

44. 45 CFR § 205.10(a) (5).

45. 22 Calif. Admin. Code §22-022.3.

46. 397 U.S. 254 (1970).

47. Yee-Litt v. Richardson, N.D. Calif, No. C-71-2287-OJC (Jan. 17, 1973).

48. "The concept underlying the new [California] regulations is that additional contact by the county worker with the recipient produces more information with which the Chief Referee makes a more informed judgment." Id., at 5.

49. 405 U.S. 208 (1972).

50. Note 121 supra, at 5.

51. Id., at 6.

52. Id.

53. Id., at 7.

54. Id., at 7-8.

55. Fair Hearing Activity from May to October 1972 Under New Fair Hearing Regulations, Memorandum from Bureau of Evaluation to Jule Sugarman, Administrator-Commissioner, New York City Human Resources Administration, Dec. 14, 1972, at 1.

56. Id., at 2.

57. Id., at 4.

58. Id., at 6.

59. Id., at 6.

60. Id.

4

ACCEPTANCE OF
ADMINISTRATIVE JUSTICE

The fair hearing process must be considered as part of the overall subject of welfare. It is not a process that lawyers can develop in splendid isolation. There are nonlegal values that will influence the interpretation of any legally imposed fair hearing criteria: (1) welfare in fact is perceived as a benefit, a gratuity, and not a right; (2) there is a limit on the dollar cost of welfare that a state will bear. At times the two nonlegal values merge. Apparently this occurred with the New York City administration in August 1972. Emotional conclusions were reached through a dollar cost argument that lacked factual support.

It is true that the fair hearing process has constitutional support in a decision from the Supreme Court. Yet it is also true that that decision is one of principle and not implementation, which—especially for AFDC fair hearings—requires administrative support at both the federal and state levels. There is every indication that that support will not be forthcoming. Most of the states are pressing, and in 1973 HEW yielded to the establishment of local rather than state evidentiary hearings, which will permit earlier benefit cutoff. And, perhaps as important, the Nixon Administration has announced a strong intent to redefine (in reality, to restrict) the role of OEO legal services. The result of that redefinition would significantly weaken OEO as the most important representative of welfare claimants. It is all too clear that without adequate representation the best fair hearing system becomes useless. Finally, through implementing regulations, HEW has caused federal auditing necessary to formulating federal payments not to reward states that fully comply with fair hearing requirements. More precisely, states will not receive federal contributing funds for improper welfare overpayments, and they will not receive credit for improper underpayments. The effect of this policy is to encourage adverse claimant action at the point of initial decision.

For all that has been said, there will be an AFDC fair hearing system that will be compelled to meet minimum constitutional standards. Even without OEO legal services, there will be some private organizational support in behalf of welfare claimants—for example, through the New York Urban Coalition. And some states will want to see the fair hearing process work. The challenge, stated in minimum terms, is to assist, to be supportive of states that seek a fair hearing mechanism responsive to the needs of claimants as well as the budget demands of the states. It is necessary to meet that challenge, for it goes to protect the basic income for more than one in twenty Americans at some point in their lives.

HEW regulations in the area of fair hearings will change as administrations change. The regulations in no small measure reflect political judgments as to the nonlegal values at issue. To an administration that sees welfare as a right, as a human need that must be met, there is apt to be greater flexibility, not only in determining eligibility but also in questions of aid continuance. To an administration that sees welfare as counterproductive to the development of a vigorous society, there are apt to be real disincentives to declaring a person eligible for welfare and to allowing aid continuance if there is a question as to continued eligibility.

It may be useful to illustrate briefly the points made. To an administration that sees welfare as a right, the determination of eligibility will likely be on the basis of claimant declaration. That is, the claimant will state qualification for welfare on a brief form; there will be few questions; welfare will be granted. To an administration that sees welfare as counterproductive of a vigorous society, self-declaration will not suffice. Investigation, detailed questioning, and time for analysis will all be allowed. Such is the thrust of the regulations promulgated by the Nixon Administration.

What has been said of eligibility determination applies as well to the formal fair hearing process. The requirements of due process will be met and often exceeded by an administration that sees welfare as a right, and exceptions to aid continuance will be narrowly drawn. No aid cutoff will be permitted until after the formal state fair hearing decision. Federal compliance techniques will be developed to insure state compliance with fair hearing requirements. But an administration that sees welfare as counterproductive will take another approach. Exceptions to aid continuance will be broadly drawn. Aid cutoff will be permitted after a local hearing. Federal compliance techniques will not be drawn broadly to insure compliance with fair hearing regulations; compliance will be left largely to the states.

The values and problems surrounding AFDC fair hearings will remain, whatever regulations are promulgated by HEW. Those regulations in several important respects have no lasting quality, for they reflect political judgments. But this is not to say that the regulations on their face can go directly against the Constitution, as interpreted by the Supreme Court, or statute, for surely for HEW to do so would be to engage in an ultra vires act. Nor do we mean to say that HEW willingly would institute administrative practices designed to subvert either the Constitution or statute. The point is simply that both the Constitution and statute are subject to interpretation. As the agency administering statute, HEW must render the initial interpretation. The nature of that interpretation is in no small way dependent on the values held by agency decision makers.

Whatever may be the factors that impel a given political judgment, administrative justice, within reasonable bounds, should take its own measure; that is, the law can accept a range for legitimate interpretation and enforcement of statute. Within that range, however, the law, to remain law, demands certain uniform standards of enforcement. So it was not at all surprising for consensus to emerge from about 70 representatives of large-population states such as New York, California, and Texas, and smaller states such as Maryland and Virginia. Consensus also seemed to come from HEW and OEO legal services and from individuals, whether Republicans or Democrats. The consensus centered around the criteria that administrative justice should demand of fair hearings. The consensus came during a three-day conference in June 1973, Mass Administrative Justice: AFDC Fair Hearings, convened by the Center for Administrative Justice of the American Bar Association.

The 70 representatives present at the conference, on the whole, held policy-making positions. The state and HEW officials present were at the level of deputy commissioner or general counsel. In-depth discussions with each other and with representatives from OEO legal services; schools of law, social work, and political science; and practicing members of the bar led to two central points of agreement:

First, not only hearing officers but also all those involved in decision making touching upon the fair hearing process should be the object of an intense educational program conducted by an impartial body such as the Center for Administrative Justice. The first goal of that educational program should be to bring decision makers in the fair hearing process to a level of minimum competence. The program should assist the decision makers in understanding the parameters of their jobs and the demands of due process. Moreover, each person should know where he stands in the total decision-making process. The result of such understanding might be not only to make the process more efficient and to bring compliance with articulated due process criteria but also to humanize the process. Individual decision makers, despite segmented job functions, might better understand that the fair hearing process itself operates with considerable impact upon individuals.

Second, an educational program would be designed to impart information and sensitivity regarding the decision-making functions attendant to the fair hearing process. It followed, according to the conference consensus, that methods should be devised to determine whether the fair hearing process performs as expected. The need, of course, is obvious. The question developed by the conference related to that need: What kind of system can be formulated to provide ongoing evaluation of the fair hearing system, particularly in the context of tens of thousands of cases each year?

Reference was made by the conference to HEW's already established quality control program applicable to determining improper payments by the states. Why couldn't a quality control program be designed to test the fair hearing process? New York City's independent office of evaluation, as shown in the study done by Donna Kirchheimer (see Appendix B) clearly indicates that such a quality program for fair hearings is possible. Indeed, the study itself, with some individual state adaptation, could well be used as it is.

Education and ongoing evaluation thus were the two recommendations emanating from the conference. Viewed in terms of furthering administrative justice, few can question these goals. The more meaningful query is whether the states or HEW will allow the principles embodied in their recommendations to be fully implemented.

But perhaps, in a broader sense, the choice is not altogether theirs. As experts, they have addressed themselves to the problem of mass administrative justice and AFDC fair hearings. Perhaps now the challenge is more clearly one put to the organized bar, and more specifically the American Bar Association. It is, after all, the members of the organized bar who have assumed a professional responsibility to society for improving the quality of justice, including administrative justice.

APPENDIX A: HEW FAIR HEARING
REQUIREMENTS

In tabular form, what follows is a comparison between HEW fair hearing regulations promulgated after Goldberg v. Kelly and the regulations as revised on August 15, 1973. The chart was prepared by the Center on Social Welfare Policy and Law. It should be noted that in the new regulations the word "fair" has been eliminated.

Items of Change in Revised Application and Determination
of Eligibility Regulations

Published August 15, 1973   38 Federal Register 22009

Old Regulation §206.10*	Changes Which Appear in New Regulation; These Changes Were Effective October 15, 1973, or Earlier if State Wished	Change from Proposal†
	Filing of Application	
(a) (1) (ii)	1) State must require a written application on a prescribed form signed under penalty or perjury as opposed to former requirement that state had to accept clear oral or written statement of intent to claim assistance (which could be later reduced to writing on form) whether submitted in person, by mail or phone. [This appears to mean, among other things, that (1) all requirements for action on applications are effective only when agency has received the written, signed, prescribed form and (2) there is no provision to insure agency action in response to oral or general written requests.]	
	2) Changes "designated representative" who may file on individual's behalf to "authorized representative." [Does this indicate agency will be able to require formal proof of authorization or otherwise establish requirements for person seeking to file application as representative of another?]	
	3) Person other than authorized representative can file only on behalf of applicant who is incompetent or incapacitated. [Although this is pointed to in the notice of rule-making as a loosening of restrictions, it is actually a limitation. The proposal would have allowed anyone to be represented by a person other than an "authorized representative."]	X
	Time Standard	
(a) (3)	1) Substitutes 45 for 30 days for outer limit on processing of applications in all cases other than disability.	
	2) Time limit runs from "date of application under the state plan." [Apparently the reference to state plan is intended to make it clear that time doesn't run until agency has received signed application on prescribed form, but see definition of application in §206.10(b).]	
	3) Expresses previously implicit requirement that time standard may "not be used as a waiting period before granting aid."	X
	Notice of Decision on Application	
(a) (4)	Revisions of sentence structure. No apparent substantive change, but clarifies requirement that adequate notice in case of denial requires a citation of the specific regulations involved.	X

*Citation to the new regulation is the same unless change is noted.
† Proposed revisions were published April 20, 1973, 38 Federal Register 9819.

Old Regulation §206.10	Changes Which Appear in New Regulation; These Changes Were Effective October 15, 1973, or Earlier if State Wished	Change from Proposal
	Date Aid Must Begin	
(a) (6)	Substitutes "assistance" for "entitlement." [Apparently this is an agency effort to deny admission of statutory entitlement to benefits, notwithstanding recognition in Goldberg v. Kelly, et al. that state and federal law create an entitlement to public assistance.]	X
(a) (6) (i)	1) Adds requirement that assistance must be paid retroactively to thirtieth day after application (sixtieth for disability) if this is earlier than date of authorization of payment, which now could be as late as 45 days after application, and if individual then met all conditions of eligibility. [Under prior 30-day processing rule, it was clear that agency had to pay retroactively to thirtieth day if it failed to act on application by that time and the individual requested a fair hearing.]	
	2) Time standard for retroactivity runs from agency's receipt of a completed application form. [Since the agency is required under (a) (3) not to delay processing, it is anomalous that HEW thinks it will take 30 days or more to process after application is completed. It would appear that this provision for retroactivity is a meaningless "plus."]	X
	Protection for Recipients' Rights—Constitution, Statute, Decency	
(a) (10)	All references to privacy, personal dignity, special action to guard against violations of rights, and examples of specific prohibited action have been deleted. [This is perhaps the clearest example of the agency's callousness. Thus the discussion of this problem in the notice of the final regulation, on p. 22007 appears to be calculated to convey the impression that the agency restored some of these safeguards for individual rights in response to the comments. Instead the agency provided for an even greater cutback than originally proposed, deleting the requirement in the proposal that the standards and methods "not result in violation of constitutional rights (and that) the agency especially guards against violations of legal rights and against entering or searching a home illegally." Apparently the agency on second thought decided that its previous signal was too subtle.]	X
	Verification of Eligibility: Primary Source/Collateral Contact	
(a) (12)	This section is entirely deleted so that there is now no federal regulatory standard or guide as to the policies or	

practices that state agencies must use in determining the need for, and establishing methods for, verification of eligibility of an applicant or continuing eligibility of a recipient. The previous federal requirements that have been so eliminated include:

1) The requirement that applicants and recipients be relied on as the primary source of information and that no contacts be made with third parties unless the individual, after request, is unable to supply the needed information and the individual has been advised of the need to contact third parties and has been offered an opportunity to consent to such request or withdraw his/her application for aid.
2) The requirement that verification of eligibility be limited to what is reasonably necessary.
3) The requirement that agency help individuals to obtain the information they need to establish their eligibility.

(a) (12) (New)

State Supervision of Local Agency Practices
Expresses requirement already expressed in 45 C.F.R. §205.100 and 205.120 that state agency supervise local agencies' adherence to state plan and procedures for determining eligibility and take corrective action where necessary.

(b) (2)

Adds requirement that application be in writing.

§205.20

Revoked. This revokes the mandatory use of the "simplified method" in the adult categories and the requirement that states work toward simplification in AFDC. [It should be noted that this provision not only related to the simplified or declaration method of determining eligibility, i.e., reliance on the individual's statements, but also contained the only regulatory requirement that states work toward simplification of the application form itself and the overall process.]

Items of Change in Revised Fair Hearing Regulations

Published August 15, 1973   38 Federal Register 22007

Old Regulation §205.10	New Regulation §205.10	Items of Change Which Appear in New Regulations; These Changes Were Effective October 15, 1973, or Earlier if State Wished	Change from Proposal*
(a)	(a)	State plan shall provide for a "system of fair hearings" changed to "system of hearings." This change continues throughout.	X
(a) (1)	(a) (1)	State agency responsibility for fair hearings changed to responsibility for (1) state agency hearing (SAH) or (2) evidentiary hearing at local level (LEH) with right of appeal. [This modifies local hearing option previously proposed at §205.10(a)(5)(ii). For effect on continuation, see especially discussion of new (a)(6).] Note: 1) State and not local agency decides whether there will be a local hearing system. 2) State may permit local hearings in some districts and not in others. 3) Both SAH and LEH must meet due process and standards prescribed in §205.10.	X
(a) (2) (a) (2) (i)	(a) (3) (a) (3) (i)	Notification of Right to Hearing Prior statement that individual be notified of right to hearing changed to notification of "right to a hearing, as provided in . . . (a)(5)." [The addition of this specificity is at least curious since grounds for a hearing are detailed in both new (a)(5) and (a)(12).]	X

---

*Proposed regulation was published April 20, 1973, 38 Federal Register 9819.

Old Regulation §205.10	New Regulation §205.10	Items of Change Which Appear in New Regulations; These Changes Were Effective October 15, 1973, or Earlier if State Wished	Change from Proposal
(iii)	(iii)	Representation by "authorized representative." [Does this mean that agency may prescribe rules as to authorization or otherwise seek to limit individual's choice? See similar change in §206.10.]	X
(iv)		Notification of any provision for payment of legal fees deleted.	X
(a)(3)	(a)(5) and (a)(12)	Opportunity for Hearing: Grounds, Scope	
(a)(3)	(a)(5)	1) Old regulation said "individual"; new regulation distinguishes between hearing rights of applicant and recipient.	X
		2) Change from "aggrieved by any other agency action affecting receipt, suspension, reduction or termination . . . or by agency policy as it affects his situation" to "aggrieved by agency action resulting in suspension, reduction, discontinuance, or termination." [This appears to eliminate requirement of opportunity for hearing where individual wishes to challenge agency action in his/her case without refusing to comply or otherwise forcing situation to a reduction or termination mode, except for those situations listed in new (a)(12).]	X
		3) Eliminates requirement of hearing on across-the-board adjustments required by change in state or federal law unless a grant computation issue is raised. [Note this refers only to state or federal law, not local policy changes. See also new group hearing policy, new (a)(5)(iv) below.]	X
(a)(3)(i)	(a)(5)(i)	1) Substitutes requirement that state may require all hearing requests to be in writing for prior rule of "any clear expression, oral or written."	
		2) Substitutes "authorized representative" for "person acting for" claimant. [See note in discussion of new (a)(3)(iii).]	X
(ii)	(ii)	Changes requirement that agency "must" help claimant submit hearing request and prepare for hearing to "may."	X
(iii)	(iii)	Specifies 90 days as outer limit on time that may be allowed for filing hearing request in lieu of former "reasonable time"; agency may still prescribe less than 90 days.	X
(a)(3)(iv) (a)	(a)(12)(i)	Deletes reference to "suspension" in describing grounds for hearing; adds "termination or reduction." [But see reference to "suspension" in new (a)(5), above.]	X
(iv) (b)		Deleted in its entirety, thereby removing explicit requirement that claimant be allowed to raise at hearing issue of agency's interpretation of the law and equitableness of promulgated policies. [Although it is anomalous to even suggest that an individual could be foreclosed from raising such issues in a hearing otherwise properly brought, it is equally obvious that HEW must have had some purpose in deleting this requirement. For one thing, its absence could allow agencies to assert that state agency interpretations and/or policies are not open to question at LEH. In any case, the general effect is to require reference to general legal principles rather than clear regulatory standard to determine scope of hearing.]	

Old Regulation §205.10	New Regulation §205.10	Items of Change Which Appear in New Regulations; These Changes Were Effective October 15, 1973, or Earlier if State Wished	Change from Proposal
(iv) (c)	(a)(12)(ii)	Deletes (4), requirement that individual be provided for hearing on "conditions of payment, including work requirements." [See discussion of new (a)(5), item 2 above. Note: Sub (3) relating to "protective payments" is retained.]	X
(a)(3)(v)	(a)(5)(iv)	Group Hearings 1) Local as well as state agencies may consolidate hearing requests where the "sole issue is one of State or Federal law or policy or changes in State or Federal law." Former regulation allowed only where "sole issue . . . is . . . agency policy." [Note state or federal, not local.] 2) Deletes individual right to withdraw from group hearing and right of recipients to request a group hearing.	X X
(vi)	(v)	Dismissal or Denial of Hearing Request 1) Permits agency to discuss or deny hearing request where sole issue is one of state or federal law requiring across-the-board grant changes. [Not clear that agency would be precluded by individual's assertion of incorrect computation in his/her case. See new (a)(5), item 3 above.] 2) Permits agency to deem hearing request "abandoned" where individual or representative fails to appear "without good cause." [This is apparently intended to delete present requirement, expressed in PRG §205.10.III.C, that agency must first contact individual and give him/her opportunity to explain no-show before treating hearing as abandoned and to allow the agency to initially assume lack of good cause absent initiation of contact by individual.]	X X
(a)(4)	(a)(2)	Deletes statement that publicity of hearing procedures be "for the guidance of all concerned."	X
(a)(5)	(a)(4)	Advance Notice of Action on Grant 1) Deletes the term "advance" throughout section and uses only the terms "timely" and "adequate" notice, with "timely" used to refer to notice before the action, i.e., the former "advance" notice concept. [This results in such contradictions in terms as providing that agency need not give "timely" notice although it must give notice by a prescribed date.] 2) Provides timely, i.e., advance, notice need not be given in exceptions listed in (a)(4)(ii) or (iii).	
(i) (A)	(i) (A)	Timely Notice 1) 15 days in advance changed to 10. 2) Required notice period now only has to precede "date of action, that is, the date upon which recipient would normally receive his assistance check" rather than former requirement that it precede the date "the action is to be taken." [This will exacerbate problem of recipient not receiving a timely payment even if he/she promptly requests hearing because the agency has not established necessary mechanism to provide for prompt issuance of check. As a practical matter, the individual who is now required to file a written hearing request would have to have that request filed well before the 10th day and/or personally appear at the welfare center on that day to be sure of receiving the check that would otherwise be due on the 10th day.]	X

Old Regulation §205.10	New Regulation §205.10	Items of Change Which Appear in New Regulations; These Changes Were Effective October 15, 1973, or Earlier if State Wished	Change from Proposal
(i) (B)	(i) (B)	Adequate Notice Changed from "details of reasons for the proposed agency action" to "a statement of what action the agency intends to take, the reasons for the intended agency action, the specific regulations supporting such action."	X
	(a) (4) (ii)	Exceptions to Timely (Advance) Notice 1) Local as well as state agency may make decision to dispense with timely (advance) notice.	X
		2) Agency must send "adequate" notice no later than "date of action." [This would apparently refer back to definition of "date of action" for timeliness, i.e., date on which individual would otherwise expect to receive check.]	X
		3) Exceptions: (A) Factual information confirming death of a recipient or of an AFDC payee. In case of AFDC payee, exception applies only where there is no relative available to serve as new payee. [Query: How can agency conclusively determine nonavailability of relative?]	X
		(B) Recipient, in writing, states no longer wishes assistance or gives information requiring change and indicates understands this is result to follow.	
		(C) Admission or commitment to institution where further assistance payments could not be federally matched.	
		(D) Placed in skilled nursing care, intermediate care, or long-term hospitalization. [What about personal needs payments, medical assistance?]	X
		(E) Whereabouts unknown and mail returned by post-office indicating no known forwarding address.	
		(F) Accepted for assistance in new jurisdiction, i.e., new state.	
		(G) AFDC child removed from home as result of judicial determination or voluntarily placed in foster care.	X
		(H) Change in level of medical care prescribed by patient's physician. [Meaning?]	X
		(I) Termination of time-limited special allowance where initiation of allowance included written notice of termination date.	X
		4) The proposed (e) and (g), likelihood of fraud and change of payee, e.g., protective payee, have been omitted. The agency has reproposed (e).	X
		5) The proposed requirement that assistance be reinstated retroactively and continued until hearing where individual requests hearing within 15 days of mailing of notice and there is a question of fact or judgment, has been deleted. Subsumed in (a) (7) which, inter alia, changes 15 to 10 and drops requirement of retroactivity.	X
	(a) (4) (iii)	Requires "timely" and "adequate" notice of across-the-board cutbacks. [This provision appears to be redundant.]	X
(a) (5) (ii)		The requirement that there be an opportunity for local conference to try to resolve problem before hearing is deleted in its entirety.	X
(a) (5) (iii) (a) (6) (a) (5) (iii) (a) (6) (i) (a) (1) and (a) (6) (i) (A)		Continuation of Assistance Pending Hearing 1) Changed from "assistance is continued" to "assistance shall not be suspended, reduced, discontinued or terminated (but is subject to recovery . . .)." [See also new §233.20 (a) (12).]	X
		2) Changes requirement of continuation "until hearing decision is rendered and through a period consistent with the State's established policies for	

Old Regulation §205.10	New Regulation §205.10	Items of Change Which Appear in New Regulations; These Changes Were Effective October 15, 1973, or Earlier if State Wished	Change from Proposal
		issuance of payments" to delete everything after "rendered." [This could mean that HEW would allow agency to prorate checks prospectively while awaiting a hearing decision, e.g., instead of issuing normal monthly check, issue weekly checks from first of month on, pending decision, although this is obviously contrary to Goldberg requirement of continuation of assistance.]	
		3) Requires continuation until hearing without regard to whether issue is one of fact, judgment, or policy. [Yee-Litt, affirmed by the Supreme Court June 5, 1973, 41 LW 3637]	X
		4) Provides assistance may be discontinued or changed prior to hearing decision if determination is made at hearing that sole issue is one of state or federal law or policy.	X
	(a)(6)(i) (B)	May make change resulting from separate action when hearing not requested after notice of change.	X
(a)(5)(iii) (a)(2)	(a)(6)(ii)	Changes requirement of notice that state agency make determination as whether continuation required to allow local agency to make decision.	
	(a)(6)(iii)	1) Assistance must be discontinued, reduced, etc. after LEH if LEH decision is unfavorable to individual, i.e., state cannot continue assistance pending review of LEH.	X
		2) Individual must be mailed written notice of adverse LEH decision which includes information that he/she can make written request for SAH within 15 days of mailing.	
		3) SAH review solely a review on record limited to determination of substantial evidence unless individual specifically requests "de novo hearing." [No specific provision that local agency advice as to right to de novo review include information as to significance. Although reference to review of substantial evidence only obviously could not mean that the state review could fail to review the correctness of the legal conclusions, it is probable that this sloppiness in drafting will lead to some state attempts to narrow scope of review. Also, no provision for LEH favorable to individual; see item 5 in discussion of (a)(15) below.]	X
(a)(5)(iii) (b)		1) Provision providing that the state may continue aid in all cases deleted in its entirety. [See (a)(6)(iii) above.]	
	(a)(7)	2) Provision that state may provide for reinstatement and continuation of assistance where a hearing request is filed within an additional specified period beyond the 15-day advance notice period changed to provide that additional period cannot be greater than 10 days after date of action (i.e., 20 days from mailing of notice) and that state cannot continue aid past hearing if it is determined that sole issue was policy or law.	X
		3) In cases where "timely", i.e., advance, notice not provided—presumably pursuant to exceptions in (a)(4)(i)—aid must be reinstated if a hearing is requested within 10 days of mailing notice of action and "the agency determines that the action resulted from other than the application of State or Federal Law." [This does not specifically require that reinstatement must be retroactive. Also apparently intended to revive general fact/ policy distinction for nonadvance notice cases and allow agency to decide prior to hearing whether question is fact or policy. Indeed provision on	X

Old Regulation §205.10	New Regulation §205.10	Items of Change Which Appear in New Regulations; These Changes Were Effective October 15, 1973, or Earlier if State Wished	Change from Proposal
		its face would deny reinstatement in all cases since presumably all actions result from application of state or federal law. However, this last is so ridiculous that it must be assumed to be sloppy drafting rather than intent.]	
(a)(6)		Requirement that information and referral services be provided to help individuals secure available legal representation deleted in entirety.	X
(a)(7)	(a)(8)	Holding of hearing at time, place, and date "convenient to claimant" changed to "reasonable."	
(a)(8)	(a)(9)	Hearing Officers. 1) Hearings may be conducted by "designee" as well as official of agency. [Does this open way for non-employees of agency to be hearing officers? If so, what provision to ensure appointment and performance consistent with general state plan requirements, e.g., confidentiality?]	X
		2) Changes from requirement that "hearing official must not have been involved in any way with the action in question" to "shall not have been directly involved in the initial determination of the action in question."	X
(a)(9)	(a)(10)	Medical Assessment where medical issue is disputed at hearing. 1) Deletes requirement that additional medical assessment be from source satisfactory to claimant.	
		2) Deletes right of appellant to request additional medical assessment for purposes of hearing.	X
(a)(10)(i)	(a)(13)(i)	Conduct of Hearing. Adds right to examine entire contents of case file prior to or during hearing.	X
	(ii)	Changes "others including legal counsel" to "authorized representative."	X
(a)(11)	(a)(16)	Final Agency Action. 1) Extends time for final agency action from 60 days to 90 days.	
		2) Deletes exception from claimant's request for delay.	X
		3) Changes 90 days from "request for a fair hearing" to "request for a hearing." [Are there now one or two 90-day periods, i.e., where LEH and SAH, does agency have 180 days or 90 days for each decision?]	X

PREFACE

This report is the product of a community evaluation effort whose aim was to examine an HRA program that was of concern to the recipients of social services. The need to evaluate the fair hearings procedures was identified by Mildred Dweck, Director of the United Welfare League (UWL), which represents public assistance recipients at the fair hearings. Ms. Dweck and Sarah Martinez, the UWL's lay advocate, aided the HRA evaluators in planning the research design so that the evaluation would address fair hearing problems that critically affect the rights of hearing appellants.

Richard Greenberg, staff attorney at the Center on Social Welfare Policy and Law, and Richard Hiller, welfare coordinator at Community Action for Legal Services, lent considerable assistance in acquainting the evaluators with the legal context of the fair hearing process and with the experiences of attorneys and paraprofessionals who represent clients at fair hearings.

HRA Administrator Jule M. Sugarman authorized members of the HRA Bureau of Evaluation to observe the fair hearings. The observers were: Andrea Burgess, Ron Butler, Julio Castro, Diane Hopsia, Nathan Hugee, and Gregory Ludd. The Bureau of Evaluation was directed by James Masters and was a unit of HRA central administration until its transfer to HRA's Department of Community Development.

The help of Florence Aitchison, associate regional commissioner for assistance payments of the Department of Health, Education and Welfare, and Elsie Seltzer, administrator of HRA's Fair Hearing

---

Note: The New York City Human Resources Administration has approved this report for publication and adds that some of the federal fair hearing regulations have been modified since the study was completed and some of the HRA operating procedures, particularly those regarding method and content of notification of clients that an action will take place, also have been modified.

Donna Kirchheimer is chief of the Community Evaluation Unit, Department of Community Development, New York City Human Resources Administration.

Section, is greatly appreciated, particularly in locating the hearing decisions as they were issued.

Valerie Leach and Stephen Leeds of the HRA Office of Policy Planning, Research and Evaluation provided crucial assistance, respectively, in statistical analysis and computer programming, and in editing the report.

INTRODUCTION

This study examines whether the fair hearing process in New York City follows the New York State Social Services Law and department regulations.[1] The findings in the report measure compliance with these regulations and are based on observations of 411 fair hearings held in October 1972.

The fair hearing is an administrative grievance procedure that must be afforded to an applicant or recipient of public assistance who contends that a law, rule, or policy has been incorrectly applied to the facts of his particular case.

The fair hearing is a formal evidentiary procedure that is conducted, under the existing regulations, by the state Department of Social Services. The hearings must afford basic due process safeguards to comport with constitutional requirements enunciated by the U.S. Supreme Court decision Goldberg v. Kelly.[2] The state regulations were modified in April 1972 to comply with the fair hearing requirements of the Department of Health, Education and Welfare[3] as a result of the U.S. Appeals Court ruling Almenares v. Wyman.[4] This study was conducted six months after the state regulatory changes became effective.

There are two general types of appeals on which fair hearings are held.

1. Appeals of agency proposals to terminate, suspend, or reduce public assistance grants. The state regulations following the Almenares decision require that clients receive 15-day prior notification of the agency's intentions and that, if a hearing request is received within the advance notice period, assistance be continued until the decision is issued.

2. Other appeals. These may regard denials of new applications or failure to act promptly; adequacy of grants or special allowances; or any other agency policy or action as it affects a particular case.

Federal fair hearing requirements apply to all categorical aid programs (Aid to Families with Dependent Children and Aid to the Aged, Blind and Disabled) to which the federal government contributes. The state regulations also extend to the nonfederal home relief cases.

The fair hearings are conducted by a state hearing officer who represents the New York State commissioner of the Department of Social Services, who formally issues the hearing decision. The claimant making the appeal may appear at the hearing alone or with a representative, attorney, lay advocate, friend, relative, or other spokesman. The city representative, who is a member of the Fair Hearings Section of the HRA income maintenance programs, presents the agency's case on the basis of evidence provided by a person from the income maintenance center, who also attends the hearing. All fair hearings on financial assistance in New York City are held at the World Trade Center in lower Manhattan.

COMMUNITY EVALUATION

A significant aspect of this study is that it was conducted as a community evaluation. The purpose of community evaluation was to examine a program of the Human Resources Administration that was of concern to a community organization representing the recipients of social services. The community organization functioned as the agency's client for the study, and in this role identified the program it felt should be evaluated and ensured that the research design would examine the program's problems as they affect and are perceived by the recipients of services.

Basic to the community evaluation approach was the agreement that results of the study would be shared with the client organization.

The community organization that identified the need to evaluate the fair hearing process and functioned as the client for this study was the United Welfare League. The UWL represents public assistance recipients at fair hearings and is funded through the Council Against Poverty and the Mid West Side Community Corporation.

METHODOLOGY

This study selected twenty sections or subsections of the state hearing regulations, which provide important procedural rights and protections for appellants, and examined whether agency actions complied with those standards.

For this purpose the evaluators drew a systematic sample of 411 appeals from the 1,177 public assistance hearings held in October 1972. The hearings in the sample were observed by members of the HRA Bureau of Evaluation, who were authorized to represent HRA Administrator Jule Sugarman. Each of the selected appellants was also interviewed before and after his hearing. The experience of each case was examined to determine whether the regulatory requirements had been met.

The results of the study are based on a stratified representative sample of fair hearings held during October 1972. Any estimates based on sample observations are subject to sample error. All findings in the study are based upon the sample drawn, and the data was tested for significance at a 95 percent confidence level.

All data presented in the body of the report have been weighted to give estimates relating to the population under discussion.

SUMMARY OF FINDINGS

The findings of the study relate to compliance with the New York State Department of Social Services regulations on fair hearings that were in effect after the April 1972 regulatory changes. In order to provide a background for the measurement of regulatory compliance, other preliminary findings that describe characteristics of the hearing population are also included.

FINDINGS RELATING TO COMPLIANCE
WITH THE STATE HEARING REGULATIONS

Prior Notification to Claimants Appealing
Agency Intentions to Discontinue, Suspend,
or Reduce Assistance

- Five percent of these appellants did not receive the mandated advance notification.

- One-fourth of the appellants who were notified were not given the required timely notice, 15 days prior to agency action.

- Two-thirds of the notified claimants were not given a notice with adequate details of the agency's reasons, as called for in the regulations.

- Twelve percent of the notification forms did not indicate that the proposed action had been reviewed by the agency, as required, to determine its correctness.

Other Procedures Applicable to Claimants Appealing Agency Intentions to Discontinue, Suspend, or Reduce Assistance

- In one of seven of the appeals that met the aid-continuing regulatory standards, the city or state agency did not continue aid as required.

- Eight percent of the appellants were automatically provided copies of the agency's documentary evidence before the hearing date. Regulations require that these documents be sent 48 hours after receipt of a hearing request.

Procedure Applicable to All Hearing Appellants

- On one-third of the hearings, the city representative was not prepared to present evidence as stipulated in the regulations.

- Fifty percent of the hearings were attended by the person from the income maintenance center responsible for the proposed agency action. Full attendance is required by regulation.

- The agency did not inform the appellants in writing, as required, of the availability of community legal services to assist them in the fair hearing.

- Agency help to appellants in preparing their cases, which regulations state should be emphasized, was provided to 5 percent of the claimants.

- When claimants made a specific request, they were afforded an opportunity prior to the hearing date to examine the agency's documentary evidence in one out of four cases.

- In cases involving health issues, two-thirds of the appellants who desired the independent medical assessment provided for in the regulations received one.

- Fifty percent of the appellants requesting reimbursement for transportation expenses received payment. Payment upon request is required by regulation.

- Less than 1 percent of appellants requesting child care and other expenses received reimbursement.

- An opportunity to cross-examine adverse witnesses was afforded at 2 percent of the hearings, where a special agency witness was present. An income maintenance supervisor or specialist familiar with the case attended 18 percent of the hearings and therefore could function, when appropriate, as an opposing witness.

- Thirty percent of the hearing decisions were issued by the state Department of Social Services after the regulatory limit of 60 days from receipt of the hearing request.

DESCRIPTION OF THE HEARING POPULATION

The largest group at the fair hearings consisted of black and Spanish-speaking women; the former accounted for 36 percent of the appellants and the latter for 26 percent. Least represented were white men, who composed only 6 percent. Other groups were: white women, 13 percent; black men, 12 percent; and Spanish-speaking men, 7 percent.

Eighty percent of the appellants represented themselves at the hearings. Eleven percent were represented by trained lay advocates and 8 percent by legal services attorneys. Also, 10 percent were accompanied by friends or relatives who acted as spokesmen, interpreters, or witnesses for the appellant.

Eighty-eight percent of the fair hearings arose from proposed agency actions to discontinue, reduce, or suspend assistance. Two-thirds of these issues regarded either check recoupment for alleged client fraud or alleged poor attendance in the Public Works Program. The remaining 12 percent concerned denials of applications, adequacy of grants, and other issues.

Fifty-three percent of the appeals were made by recipients of aid to families with dependent children, although AFDC cases compose 72 percent of the public assistance caseload. Home relief cases were overrepresented at the hearings, and composed one-third of the appeals, although only about one-tenth of the welfare caseload. This is probably due to the high incidence of hearings pertaining to the

Public Works Project, in which home relief participation is substantial. Appeals from recipients of aid to the aged, blind, and disabled accounted for about one-sixth of the fair hearings, approximately the same proportion that AABD cases represent in the overall caseload.

Results of the hearings showed that 52 percent of the decisions issued by the state commissioner upheld the agency: 27 percent favored the appellant; and on 21 percent the city withdrew its proposed action and therefore the decision read "no issue." These proportions remained about the same for hearings held on proposed discontinuances, on check recoupments, and on other reductions. The agency was upheld for 38 percent of the hearings concerning denial of applications, and for 48 percent of the appeals in which the client challenged the adequacy of the grant; the agency rarely withdrew on cases of denial or adequacy.

FINDINGS: COMPLIANCE WITH FAIR HEARING REGULATIONS

Notification
Notice of Right to a Hearing
Section 358.3a-c:
Applicants and recipients of public assistance shall be informed in writing . . . at the time of any action affecting receipt of assistance or services:
    (a) of his right to a fair hearing;
    (b) of the method by which he may obtain a hearing;
    (c) that he may be represented by legal counsel, or by a relative, friend, or other spokesman, or he may represent himself

Findings

Five percent of the claimants at the fair hearings who were appealing agency actions affecting their grants stated that they had not received a notice informing them of their right to a hearing. These clients requested a hearing when their usual public assistance check did not arrive, and they found out at their income maintenance center that their grants had been terminated. (A sample of hearing appellants might, of course, be expected to have a high rate of receipt of the advance notice; it tends to be a self-selecting group on this issue.)

Two percent of those appealing changes in grants were filing affidavits on the notification issue before a federal magistrate under the Almenares v. Wyman decision.

Sufficient explanation of the client's right to representation at the hearing was not clearly stated on the advance notice form (M3c) used by the agency: "At the hearing, you, your attorney or other representative will have an opportunity to present relevant written and oral evidence against you."

Written Notice of Availability of Community Legal Services
Section 358.3(d):
Applicants and recipients of public assistance shall be informed in writing at the time of any action affecting receipt of assistance or services:
> (d) of the availability of the community legal services available to assist him in the fair hearing.

Findings

None of the appellants had been informed of the availability of community legal services in writing at the time of agency action affecting their grants. The advance notice form did not include this information.

Appellants interviewed in the study were asked whether they had been verbally told of the availability of community legal services. More than four-fifths (83 percent) responded that they had not been informed. The remainder said the city or state Department of Social Services had told them they could bring legal counsel, although not always where or how to contact free legal services. (This information was sometimes received from the state when appellant phoned to request a hearing.)

Advance Notice of Proposed Actions
(1) Timely and Adequate Advance Notice:
Section 358.8(a):
In cases of any proposed action to terminate, suspend or reduce assistance, timely and adequate advance notice thereof detailing the reasons for the proposed action shall be sent to the recipients. Under this requirement:
> 1. "Timely" means that the notice is mailed at least 15 days before the action is to be taken.
> 2. "Adequate advance notice" means a written notice that includes details of reasons for the proposed action.

Findings: Timely Notice

Five percent of the hearing appellants on issues of proposed termination, reduction, or suspension stated that they had not received any prior notification.

Twenty-one percent of the advance notices received were dated fourteen days or less prior to the agency's intended action, and an additional 4 percent were undated.

Findings: Adequate Notice

New York State and New York City regulations state that the advance notice should (1) record in detail the reasons for the proposed action, (2) give a brief description leading to the action taken, (3) record all evidence supporting the decision, (4) cite procedures or memoranda that are pertinent, and (5) include both old and new budgets if necessary to clarify the situation.

Advance notices received by appellants were examined and graded by these standards. If one or two of the details listed above were included, the notice was rated "poor"; if three or four of the required details were given, the notice was assigned an "adequate" rating. If all five details were given, or if only the pertinent regulatory citation was omitted, the notice received a "thorough" grade.

Utilizing these standards:

●Almost two-thirds (63 percent) of the notices were rated "poor." (These included 1.3 percent on which the reasons were illegibly written or were left blank.)

●About one-quarter (24 percent) were graded "adequate."

●Twelve percent were found to be "thorough."

Examples of reasons rated "poor" included: "Refused service at New York State Employment Service"; "Your husband is working and living in the household with you"; "Duplication of funds—Check dated 3/1/72"; "Concealed assets and job denial from 11/69 to 8/70"; "Failed to report to job referral on 7/19/72"; "Nonreport of employment income for your wife, Carmen"; "Excess of absences from your public works assignment"; "You have people not on public assistance sharing your apartment and contributing to your rent"; "We are closing your case at your request"; "Failure to cooperate"; and "Failure to report to Family Court."

Generally, no other written summary or documentary evidence on the agency's proposed action was seen by the claimant until the hearing commenced.

Agency notices of proposed recoupment of checks alleged to be fraudulently cashed accounted for 82 percent of the notices rated as "thorough." Only these notices tended to follow a form statement, leaving the facts particular to the case to be filled in:

It has been determined that the check of — in the amount
of — which you reported lost, stolen, or undelivered and
which was replaced by this department has been signed
and cashed by you. Your budget allowance will therefore
be reduced in the sum of — commencing with the check
of —, so that the full amount of overpayment will be
recovered in the next — semi-monthly payments.

Notices on all other reasons for proposed termination or reduction generally gave a poor explanation of the agency's action. For
example, 73 percent of the notices regarding Public Works Project
issues were graded as "poor," and 76 percent of the notices regarding
source of income or assets received a "poor" grade.

Check recoupment for alleged client fraud and terminations of
public assistance due to "failure to report" or "excessive absences"
from the Public Works Projects each accounted for about one-third
of the advance notices received by hearing appellants.

Other reasons for agency actions accounted for the following
proportions of the advance notices: source of income (employment
of client, spouse, or parents, or OASDI or unemployment insurance
benefits), 15 percent; assets (car or house ownership, inheritance,
savings, etc.), 4 percent; eligibility (school enrollment, absence of
family members, utility or rent allowances), 5 percent; cases not
notified under regulations prior to April 1972 (whereabouts unknown,
at client's request, reclassification), 2 percent; failure to comply
with regulations (did not return declaration of continued need, did not
keep court or other appointments, or "failure to cooperate"), 9 percent; and blank or illegible, 3 percent.

(2) Agency Review of Proposed Changes in Grant: Signature by
     Income Maintenance Supervisor
     Section 358.9:
     When a social services official proposes to discontinue, sus-
     pend or reduce a grant of assistance, he or his designee who
     has the appropriate authority shall review or cause to be
     reviewed the proposed action and determine its correctness.

Findings

New York City income maintenance regulations state that the
group or section income maintenance supervisor "approves and signs
that Form M3c is complete and accurate and that proposed action is
valid."

Of the M3c advance notices examined, 12 percent were not
signed by an income maintenance supervisor, and an additional 2
percent had a supervisor's name typed or stamped in. This would

indicate that one out of eight proposed agency actions was not reviewed by supervisory personnel.

In addition, on 15 percent of the M3c forms, no signature of an income maintenance specialist appeared, and another 4 percent bore a typed or stamped name. This means a total of one-quarter of the M3c notices were missing the signature of either the income maintenance supervisor or specialist.

Nine percent of the advance notices were not signed by either an income maintenance supervisor or a specialist. Fifty-four percent of the unsigned notices gave rise to hearings for which the city representative was not prepared because adequate evidence was not contained in the center's case folder. (Of the notices signed by either the supervisor or the specialist, 33 percent led to hearings for which the city representative lacked adequate evidence.)

Notice of Scheduled Hearing
Section 358.11:
At least six working days prior to the date of the hearing, written notice thereof shall be sent to the parties and their representatives informing them of rights and procedures.

Findings

The state Department of Social Services sent written notice of a scheduled hearing to the appellant and the city Fair Hearing Section at least six working days prior to the hearing date in almost all cases, as follows:

Five working days or less	5.1%
Six to ten working days	84.8%
Eleven or more working days	10.0%

Procedures Prior to Hearing
Agency Help to Appellants
Section 358.5(b):
Emphasis must be on helping the appellant to submit and process his case and in preparing his case, if needed.

Findings

Appellants were asked whether the Department of Social Services helped them at any time to prepare their cases, and 95 percent responded, "No."

A question on the client's experience at the income maintenance center showed that 60 percent of the hearing appellants had received little or no information at the center to further explain the agency's action beyond the statement given on the advance notice. (Eighty-six percent of the appellants stated that they, or their representatives, had contacted their income maintenance center after learning of the agency's proposed change in grant.)

Of the others, 7 percent were told to ask for a fair hearing, 11 percent said that adequate information was provided, and the remainder requested and/or attended conferences.

Aid Continued
Section 358.8(c 1):
In cases in which there is a request for a fair hearing within the advance notice period, assistance shall be continued until the fair hearing decision is rendered . . . except when the recipient requests an adjournment or fails to appear for the hearing without good cause.

Findings

About two-thirds (68 percent) of the appellants at the fair hearings were designated by the state Department of Social Services as aid-continuing cases. This represents 73 percent of the hearing appeals arising from M3c notices of discontinuance, reduction, or suspension of grants.

This study found, however, that 12 percent of the clients who met the aid-continuing requirements were not designated by the state to be aid-continuing as of the hearing date.

Hearing decisions by the state commissioner also indicate an error rate regarding the implementation of the aid-continuing provision. In addition to judging the hearing issue itself, the decisions found in 15 percent of the cases that aid should have been continued but had not been, and made the correction. (This includes both state and city errors.)

Documentary Evidence: Appeals of Discontinuance, Reduction, or Suspension
Section 358.9(d):
When a social services official (City agency) proposes to discontinue, suspend or reduce a grant, he or his designee who has the appropriate authority shall within 48 hours after receipt of notification of a request for a fair hearing, send to the appellant, his representative, and the Department [State DSS] copies of all documents to be submitted into evidence at the hearing in support of the proposed action.

Findings

Almost all (92 percent) of the clients appealing agency actions affecting their grants reported that they had not at any time before the hearing been provided, without special request, with copies of documents the agency planned to submit as evidence.

This finding indicates that the agency had not established administrative procedures to automatically provide documentary evidence to recipients appealing agency actions.

Documentary Evidence: All Appellants

Section 358.12a, b:

If copies of documentary evidence which the social services official plans to use at the hearing have not already been provided to the appellant, an opportunity to examine such documents, if requested, shall be afforded the appellant or his representative at a reasonable time before the date of the hearing. The recipient or his representative shall be afforded an opportunity to examine the case record at a reasonable time before the hearing to the extent permitted by Section 357.3(c) ("Particular extracts shall be furnished him, or furnished to a person whom he designates, when the provision of such information would be beneficial to him. The case record, or any part of it, admitted as evidence in the hearing of an appeal shall be open to him and his representative.")

Findings

Three-quarters of the appellants who requested to examine documentary evidence or the case record were not provided an opportunity to do so at any time before the date of the hearing. The following table shows the relationship between requesting to see documents and receiving an opportunity to examine them. If an appellant did not make a request, he had a one-in-thirteen (7.4 percent) chance of being shown the documents; if he made a special request, his chances were one-in-four (24.6 percent).

The table also indicates that only 10.5 percent of the appellants requested to examine documents the agency planned to use. Moreover, 7.9 percent of all appellants had requested to see documents and were not given the opportunity before the day of the hearing.

As found in the subgroup of discontinuances, suspensions, and reductions covered in Section 358.9(d), few (9.2 percent) in the total group of appellants examined opposing documentary evidence prior to the hearing date (including appellants making special requests).

Was Appellant Shown Documents Before Hearing Day?	Did Appellant Request to See Documents?		Total, All Appellants
	Requested Documents	Did Not Request	
No: never saw documents before hearing day	56.5%	90.2%	86.8%
No: saw documents only while waiting for hearing	18.9% } 75.4%	2.4% } 92.6%	4.0% } 90.8%
Yes: saw documents before hearing day	24.6%	7.4%	9.2%
	100.0%	100.0%	
Total: all appellants	10.5%	89.5%	100.0%

There was no indication that an administrative routine existed to make documentary evidence available at the request of appellants, before the hearing date.

A significant difference was found between appellants with trained representatives and those without, with respect to requesting and examining the agency's documentary evidence. Of the appellants with trained representatives, 26 percent requested to examine the documentary evidence, while 5 percent of the appellants who were alone or accompanied by friends or relatives made such a request. Of the claimants with trained representation, 15 percent were afforded an opportunity to see the documents in the waiting room before the hearing was called; 3 percent of the other claimants saw the documentary evidence at this time. No significant difference was found for examining the documentary evidence prior to the hearing day.

Independent Medical Assessment
Section 358.16(e):
When the hearing involves medical issues, provision shall be made to obtain a medical assessment other than that of the person(s) involved in making the original decision from a source satisfactory to the appellant if the hearing officer or the appellant deems it necessary.

Findings

About 25 percent of the hearing appeals involved issues related to health.

Almost two-thirds (64 percent) of these appellants brought a written medical report from a source that was satisfactory to the appellant.

The remaining appellants with health issues (35 percent) had not had an independent medical assessment made, although they were dissatisfied with the agency's estimation of their medical condition. Some of these appellants brought a doctor's prescription or a clinic appointment form to try to substantiate their claims. The observers did not judge these to be medical assessments.

Conduct of Hearings
Agency Help to Appellants
(1) City Representative
Section 358.9:

Responsibility of the social services official in cases of proposed discontinuance, suspension or reduction of assistance:

When a social services official proposes to discontinue, suspend or reduce a grant of assistance, he or his designee who has the appropriate authority shall take such action as is necessary to assure that an appropriate representative of the agency will appear at the hearing with the case record and a brief written summary of the agency's case and be prepared to present evidence in support of the proposed action, including: the appropriate case number and the applicable category or categories of public assistance or care; the names, addresses, relationships and ages of persons affected, the decision or action which prompted the request for the fair hearing; a brief description of the facts, evidence and reasons allegedly supporting such decision or action, including identification of the specific provisions of law, department regulations and approved local policies which allegedly support the proposed action; the relevant budget or budgets prepared by the social services district for the person or family.

Findings

The city representative was prepared to present evidence at about one-third (35 percent) of the hearings held on proposed discontinuances, reductions, and suspensions.

About half of the cases for which the city representative was unprepared went to a full hearing. (This equals one-sixth of all hearings.) The other half were withdrawn by the city. Withdrawals for lack of evidence accounted for 81 percent of all the city representatives' decisions to withdraw proposed agency actions.

Using standards in city and state regulations, observers found the agency unprepared when relevant documentary evidence was missing, such as the client's budget or employment record; the M3c notice; a duplicate check with appellant's alleged signature.

Each of the 22 city representatives handled an average of four to five cases of day; they based their positions on case records brought to them the day of the hearing by the income maintenance center representative.

The city representative presented a brief written description (other than the advance notice) of the facts, evidence, and reasons allegedly supporting the agency's action at 48 percent of the hearings. At 52 percent of the hearings, the city representative did not present such a case extract.

Attendance of Income Maintenance Center Representatives
Section 358.9(g):
The person who made the determination to discontinue, suspend or reduce assistance or who is responsible therefor, shall appear at the hearing.

Findings

Of the hearings held on issues of discontinuance, suspension, or reduction, 30 percent had no income maintenance center representative present, and in 20 percent the income maintenance center representative stated that he was not familiar with the appellant's case and was not responsible for the agency's proposed action.

Representatives of the centers' fair hearings and conferences sections represented the centers at about one-third (32 percent) of the hearings, reflecting the recent creation or expansion of these sections in the centers.

The remaining 18 percent of the hearings were attended by the person who had made or was directly responsible for the agency's proposed determination (the income maintenance specialist or supervisor or the employment specialist).

The identity of the center's representative (responsible for the case or not; hearing section member; or absent) showed no relationship to the outcome of the decisions. Those hearings unattended by a center representative did not show a greater tendency for the city to withdraw, contrary to what might be expected. In fact, of the hearings the agency won, the largest single group (34 percent) were hearings held without a center representative present. This suggests that the training and experience of the city representative is adequate to represent the agency, and that the agency presentation does not rely on the center representative.

Appellants' Expenses
Section 358.10:
If requested, necessary transportation for the appellant and his representative and witnesses, child care and other costs and expenditures reasonably related to the hearing is provided.

Findings

About half (49 percent) of the appellants requesting reimbursement for travel expenses were provided with payment. However, less than a third (29 percent) of the appellants made requests for travel reimbursement.

None of the claimants who requested reimbursement for child care or other expenses received payment at the hearings. (Less than 1 percent requested and received these payments later, at the income maintenance center, based on the postcard follow-up.)

In any case, few appellants requested payment—5 percent requested child care costs and 3 percent other reimbursement. The need for child care expenses is indicated by the facts that half the appellants are AFDC clients, about 10 percent of adjournments requested by claimants are for child care problems, and children are often brought to the hearings. The need for reimbursement for lunch expenses is indicated by the fact that 28 percent of the appellants wait through lunch hour (12 noon to 1 p.m.) for their hearings to be called.

Adverse Witnesses
Section 358.16c:
Each party has a right to testify, to produce witnesses to testify . . . to cross-examine opposing witnesses [and] to offer evidence in rebuttal.

Findings

In 2 percent of the hearings, the city agency presented an opposing witness other than the income maintenance specialist or supervisor responsible for the case. These hearings related to Public Works Project issues and agency allegations of source of income or "hidden assets."

Only 18 percent of the hearings were attended by an income maintenance center representative who was personally familiar with the case and might function as a witness for the agency.

In check duplication cases, expert testimony was rarely presented by the agency to attempt to substantiate that it was the client's own signature endorsing the duplicated check. Less than 2 percent of the city's cases alleging check fraud included a notarized statement from its expert qualified in handwriting. Personal expert testimony was never presented, and upon subpoena the city would routinely withdraw its allegation.

Verbatim Record
Section 358.16(g):
A verbatim record of the hearing shall be made.

Findings

In almost one-quarter (22.5 percent) of the hearings, the hearing officer stopped the recorder and proceedings were conducted off the record. In 3 percent, citations of law or regulations by the appellant or his representative were ruled off the record.

Hearing Decision
Section 358.18(a):
The Fair Hearing decision is made and issued by the State Commissioner on the basis of the hearing record including the recommendation of the hearing officer. It is issued within 60 days from the date the fair hearing request is received by the department. However, such time may be extended when the appellant requests a delay in his hearing.

Findings

About 70 percent of the commissioner's decisions were issued in 60 days or less from receipt of the appellant's request—excluding hearings that had been adjourned for any reason at the appellant's request. (If hearings adjourned by appellants are included in the sample, two-thirds—64 percent—were issued in 60 days. All other proportions discussed here remained the same ± one percent, whether appellant adjournments were included or excluded.)

The speed with which the hearing decisions were issued tended to change according to the content of the decision and whether the case was aid-continuing.

●Decisions stating, "There is no issue to be decided," which accepted the city's withdrawal of the proposed action, were dispatched with least delay and 91 percent of the "no issues" were out in 60 days or sooner.

●Decisions that upheld the agency ranked second in speed. Two-thirds of these were issued within the 60-day limit; 17 percent of the decisions upholding the agency were issued in over 90 days.

●Decisions reversing the agency were slowest to be issued. About half the reversals (54 percent) were released in 60 days or sooner. More than one-quarter (28 percent) took longer than 90 days.

●Six percent of the decisions in the sample had not been received by the city's Fair Hearing Section or by HEW Region 2 by the study's closing date on this question, about 200 days from the appellants' hearing requests.

●Cases that had been designated aid-continuing received decisions more quickly than other cases—71 percent of the aid-continuing cases were decided within 60 days, whereas 45 percent of the non-aid-continuing cases were decided within that limit. A greater disparity between appeals with and without aid continued existed for decisions issued within 30 days: 54 percent of those with aid continued were out in this time, in contrast to 15 percent of those without aid continued. Finally, more decisions on non-aid-continuing cases (42 percent of these) were issued in over 90 days than on aid-continued appeals (18 percent of these).

●Decisions by the state commissioner on appeals from claimants with professional or paraprofessional representatives tended to be issued more slowly than on appeals from clients alone or clients represented by friends or relatives. Of the decisions on cases with trained representatives, 38 percent were issued in over 60 days, whereas 28 percent of the decisions on appeals from claimants alone, or with friends, exceeded the 60-day regulatory limit. (Hearings adjourned for any reason on request from the appellant or his representative are excluded.)

FINDINGS: DESCRIPTION OF
HEARING CHARACTERISTICS

The following sections on conferences and adjournments relate to optional regulations, in contrast to the mandatory regulatory requirements that were reviewed in the preceding sections. Findings on waiting room time are included in this section also; waiting time is not specifically mentioned by the regulations.

Waiting Room Time

Waiting room time is a general measurement of problems related to Section 358.10 of the regulations, which states, "The hearing is held at a time and place convenient to the appellant as far as practicable."

About one-quarter of the appellants waited three and a half hours or more from the scheduled hour of their hearing to the time it was called. Appellants scheduled for 10 a.m. hearings waited the longest, more than one-quarter of them for four and a half hours or more. About 40 percent of appellants scheduled for morning hearings had to wait through the lunch hour (12 noon to 1 p.m.) for their hearings to be called.

Appellants with professional or paraprofessional representatives tended to wait longer hours than claimants who brought friends or represented themselves: 22 percent of appellants with trained representatives waited four and a half hours or more; 9 percent of other appellants waited four and a half hours or more. Also, 11 percent of appellants with trained representatives had hearings called in one hour or less, and 25 percent of other claimants waited less than an hour.

The waiting time also affects the income maintenance center representatives, who otherwise would complete their hearings and return to the centers.

Long waiting periods are probably due to the large number of hearings scheduled and held, and to the number of cases per hearing officer, rather than to the duration of each hearing. An average of 58 hearings was held every day, approximately 10 per hearing officer. Excluding city withdrawals, which were generally handled in less than 15 minutes, 20 percent of the hearings were conducted in 15 minutes or less; 44 percent in 15 to 30 minutes; 16 percent in half an hour to 45 minutes; 6 percent in 46 to 60 minutes; and 15 percent in over one hour.

Conferences

The public assistance recipient's right to a conference is provided in Section 358.8(b) of the New York State regulation:

> If, within the advance notice period, the recipient indicates his wish for a conference with local agency staff, an opportunity shall be provided for the recipient (or his representative) to discuss his situation with appropriate local agency staff, obtain an explanation of the reasons

101

for the proposed action, and present information to show
that the proposed action is incorrect.

This study found that almost one-quarter of the hearing appellants on issues of termination, reduction, or suspension of grants had
previously had conferences at their income maintenance centers. Two
percent had requested conferences that had not yet been held by the
day of the fair hearing.

Holding a conference prior to the hearing showed no relationship to the outcome of the hearing decision; that is, cases on which
conferences had been previously held were decided in roughly the
same proportions—25 percent agency reversals, 50 percent agency
upheld, and 25 percent city withdrawals—as cases without prior conferences. It was expected that hearing appeals in cases where prior
conferences had been decided against the client would have a higher
proportion of hearing decisions against the appellants than hearings
appeals in cases where there had been no prior conference.

Recalling the pattern of issues giving rise to fair hearings,
check fraud and Public Works Project issues were the principal causes
for holding conferences. (Half the conferences were held on check
recoupments and one-quarter on terminations of PWP enrollees.)

Internal procedures at the conferences apparently did not provide the claimant with a complete knowledge of the evidence against
him. This is indicated by the fact that three-quarters of the appellants who had conferences stated that they had not seen the agency's
documentary evidence prior to the hearing date. In addition, only 14
percent of fair hearing claimants attending conferences had been
automatically shown documentary evidence without making a special
request.

In the context of fair hearing procedures, however, hearing
appellants who had had prior conferences accounted for a dispro-
portionately high percentage of the instances in which the hearing
appellants were afforded an opportunity to examine the agency's
evidence before the hearing date. Bearing in mind that only 9 percent
of the hearing appellants saw the documentary evidence, of those
appellants who did examine the documents before the hearing day,
almost half (44 percent) had a conference. Of those who were shown
documents without a special request, more than a third (40 percent)
had had conferences.

Adjournments

Section 358.16(f) of the state regulations permits adjournment
of a scheduled hearing: "The hearing may be adjourned by the hearing

officer for good cause on his own motion or at the request of either party."

This study found that almost one-third (32 percent) of the hearings had been adjourned from the date originally scheduled. Sixty-three percent of the adjournments had been requested by the appellant, 22 percent by the city representative, and 15 percent by the state officer.

When the same case was adjourned two times or more, it was most often at the initiative of the city or state. Of the adjournments at appellants' request, 6 percent were adjourned two or more times; 10 percent of the city adjournments were rescheduled two or more times; and 21 percent of the state adjournments were multiple.

Causes for the adjournments in the sample by appellants were: sickness, 37 percent; could not get counsel, 13 percent; child care problems, 10 percent; and transportation problems (got lost, arrived late), 40 percent. The city agency requested adjournment generally when the income maintenance staff was unprepared or the case record was missing (80 percent of the city adjournments). The state's reason for initiating an adjournment was most frequently lack of time on the calendar.

RECOMMENDATIONS

The New York City Human Resources Administration should support the existing state (18 NYCRR Part 358) and federal (45 CFR 205.10) requirements governing fair hearings, which have been in effect in New York since April 1972.

●HRA should implement the procedures set forth in the New York State fair hearing regulations, and in particular:

1. Fifteen-day advance notice should be sent, conveying thorough details on the reasons and regulatory grounds for the agency's proposed actions. Form notices should be developed on recurrent reasons and specific facts.

2. The advance notice form should clearly, and in English and Spanish, inform the recipient of community legal services and how to contact them.

3. HRA should plan and put into practice administrative procedures to automatically mail to appellants copies of documentary evidence or material from the case record the city intends to use at hearings on discontinuances, reductions, and suspensions.

4. Income maintenance centers should provide copies of documents and materials from the case record upon request by any hearing appellant.

5. Payment of travel expenses should be made at the hearing site to all appellants and their representatives when hearings are held or adjourned. Payment should be provided at the hearing site for child care and lunch expenses when necessary.

●Fair hearing procedures should be monitored every six months for compliance with regulations. The state agency responsible for the program is responsible under federal requirements for the fulfillment of fair hearing provisions. The city agency should, however, regularly monitor in particular those aspects of the hearings process for which it carries local administrative responsibility.

●HRA should establish an ombudsman service at the site of the fair hearings to provide professional or paraprofessional representatives to appellants who want representation but were unable to obtain it. The ombudsman service should act as a watchdog for the rights and interests of the hearing appellants. Cost of legal counsel to represent clients at fair hearings may receive federal financial participation available under 45 CFR 205.10.

●The city representatives at the site of the fair hearings and the fair hearings and conferences staff members in the income maintenance centers should receive thorough training in the rights of appellants preceding and during hearings. City representatives should have the responsibility and authority to ensure that the appellants' procedural rights are carried out, including payment of expenses, examination of documentary evidence, and provision of independent medical assessments when necessary.

●City representatives should withdraw the city's action when required procedures are not implemented. They should withdraw the action with prejudice when the case record provided by the income maintenance representative does not contain documentary evidence adequate to support the proposed agency action.

●The city Fair Hearing Section director should jointly plan and coordinate the responsibilities of the city representatives with the chief state hearing officer in order to develop an efficient method for handling the daily calendar and minimize waiting time for appellants, city, and income maintenance center representatives. Adequate office space, telephones, desks, and office machines should be obtained.

●Compliance by the income maintenance centers with the state commissioner's decisions should be enforced and monitored.

●Income maintenance programs should, in cooperation with the HRA general counsel's office, review and improve standards for documentary evidence required to substantiate the agency's actions on an issue-by-issue basis. City representatives should enforce these standards and record in their case folders what evidence was presented at the hearing. Of particular importance is the need to improve standards for evidence of allegations of check fraud and to identify client signatures.

●The high proportion of home relief cases and Public Works Project issues at the hearings indicates a need to review the standards for termination from PWP and, therefore, from public assistance.

NOTES

1. 18 (NYCRR Part 358).
2. 397 U.S. 254 (1970).
3. 45 C.F.R. 205.10.
4. 453 F. 2d 1075 (2d Cir. 1971), cert. denied 405 U.S. 944.

DANIEL J. BAUM is Professor of Law and Administrative Studies at the Osgoode Hall Law School of York University in Toronto, Canada. He is editor-in-chief of the Administrative Law Review, organ of the Administrative Law Section, American Bar Association.

Dr. Baum was director of the Mass Justice project of the Center for Administrative Justice, and consultant to the Administrative Conference of the United States. His most recent publication is The Final Plateau: The Betrayal of Our Senior Citizens (1974).

Dr. Baum holds a B.A. and LL.B. from the University of Cincinnati, and an LL.M. and J.S.D. from New York University.

THE IMPACT OF FEDERAL ANTIPOVERTY
POLICIES
Charles Brecher
Foreword by Eli Ginzberg

LEGAL AID AND WORLD POVERTY: A Survey
of Asia, Africa, and Latin America
Committee on Legal Services to
the Poor in Developing Countries

NEW DIRECTIONS IN EMPLOYABILITY:
Reducing Barriers to Full Employment
edited by David B. Orr

THE SOCIAL COSTS OF HUMAN UNDER-
DEVELOPMENT: Case Study of Seven New
York City Neighborhoods
Marvin Berkowitz

SOCIAL SECURITY DISABILITY AND MASS
JUSTICE: A Problem in Welfare Adjudication
Robert G. Dixon, Jr.

WORK OR WELFARE? Factors in the Choice
for AFDC Mothers
Mildred Rein